Common Sense Selling

Common Sense Selling

by
Anthony E. Pattiz

VANTAGE PRESS
New York • Los Angeles

DEDICATION

To Jill and Joan Pattiz. Two great ladies to whom I owe so much.

Contents

Common Sense Selling

What this book is not about.

This book is not intended to dramatically change your life. I have not uncovered some secret formula or hidden concept which will enable you to become wealthy beyond your wildest dreams. I am neither a P.hD. graduate of the Harvard Business School nor am I someone who has managed to amass a small fortune in a short period of time. I will not make any incredible claims nor will I guarantee anything I have written because I have learned that, in life, there are no guarantees.

Like yourself, I have browsed bookstores and seen book after book written by someone who claims to have discovered a new way to build a fortune. Some authors are even so bold as to guarantee success or refund your money—provided you follow their step-by-step approach. In their books, however, these authors cleverly claim that you cannot succeed unless you follow their step-by-step approach precisely. Any deviation, however slight, could prove disastrous.

If you are like myself, as you read between the lines, the fantastic promises begin to unravel. You start to shake your head and ask yourself, "Is this person for real?" or "Does this program really make sense for me?" As one who has read his share of "How To" books and listened to his share of "You Can" tapes, I will never forget the words of one wise speaker whom I was fortunate to hear. I was watching a program on television which dealt with the topic of how one could amass a great fortune by investing in stocks and bonds. Midway through his discussion of wealth-building strategies, this wise individual paused. He then gazed into the camera and uttered the following words, "Let's face it folks, who knows whether the program I am presenting to you this evening will really work? If I were sure, then I would be on my luxurious yacht somewhere in the Caribbean instead of trying to sell this program to you."

There you have it! While the men and women who claim to have discovered a new way to make you rich may have indeed profited from these claims, their preoccupation with selling you their "success strategies" should make you skeptical. Is their goal to build a fortune by using the program they outline in their books, tapes and seminars? Or is their goal to build a fortune by selling you their books, tapes and seminars?

The speaker whose words of wisdom I cited above reminds me of another wise man who lived from 551 to 479 B.C. His name was Confucius. He was a Chinese sage and philosopher. He wrote:

The Master said, He who learns but does not think is lost! He who

1

thinks but does not learn is in great danger!

Over two thousand years later, two men wrote a book which arrived at a similar conclusion. These men were Thomas J. Peters and Robert H. Waterman, Jr. Their book was entitled *In Search of Excellence*. As a student of business, I witnessed how this book, based on lessons from America's best-run companies, created a revolution in academic thinking at our nation's colleges and universities. Years later, after I had left a successful career with a fortune 500 firm to start my own company, I realized why this book was so important and so influential. *In Search of Excellence* had a message which was simple, yet profound. It was based on what I would describe as "Common Sense Management." The lessons learned by America's best-run companies were learned through a combination of on-the-job experience and a common sense approach to problem solving.

The companies which Peters and Waterman researched were confronted with tremendous challenges in their respective marketplaces. Their common sense approach to problem solving was tempered by the experience they gained as they matured. The men and women who built these great institutions and their successors did not discover a secret formula or a hidden concept which empowered them to change their business environments overnight. They succeeded because they were able to develop a series of strategies and techniques which they applied to their organizations and their customers. These strategies and techniques—while having a profound impact on their success—were simple and straightforward. And, as their markets changed, America's best-run companies possessed the flexibility to change as well.

This is not a book about America's best-run companies. This is a book about the lessons I learned while managing a business of a smaller size and scope. These lessons do not focus on all aspects of managing a business or working for others who manage a business. My background is in sales and marketing. I have had seven years of training and experience in selling products and satisfying customers. Therefore, I consider this to be my greatest strength. My story is about the process I developed to create an opportunity to sell my products and satisfy my customers. I call this process: **Common Sense Selling**.

Common Sense Selling is written for anyone whose job is to sell a product or a service—whether you own a business or work for someone else. This book is written for anyone who is interested in creating a clientele and satisfying that clientele. I do not profess to offer any million dollar insights or provide a compendium of scholarly writings in the field of marketing. The words in this book are mine and the insights are those which I acquired as I attempted to transform a start-up business into a profitable enterprise.

When I started my business, I had no customers and no revenues. Twelve months later, I had reached the threshold of profitability. During this period, I amassed no great fortunes nor uncovered any revolutionary ideas. What I succeeded in accomplishing through the application of certain basic yet powerful ideas was to build a viable customer base and a proven cash flow where none had previously existed. The story which unfolds is what I learned and how I was able to apply these lessons to my business environment.

My common sense approach to selling has many features. You may decide to adopt all of them or only a few. What is important is that these concepts can be embraced as a whole or individually if you so desire. It is my hope that you will emerge from this book with at least one idea which you can use to make a difference in your business or profession.

During his nation's darkest hour of peril, Winston Churchill appealed to America to assist him in his struggle against Nazi tyranny. He said, "Give us the tools and we will do the job." *Common Sense Selling* offers you the tools. The rest is up to you.

Let's take a look at the big picture.

Before discussing specific strategies for building your customer base, I believe it is important to examine the larger arena in which you operate. Whether you are the owner of a business or work for someone else, it is important to understand that selling is only one part of your overall operation. While you might have the world's most effective sales campaign, you may still fail as a result of other factors which influence your business. In this chapter, we will briefly examine some of these other factors.

Webster's New Collegiate Dictionary defines selling as:

Persuading or influencing to a course of action or to the acceptance of something...

This definition implies persuading your prospect that he or she needs your product (or service) based on its ability to fill a perceived need or set of needs. You, as we shall later see, are responsible for managing your prospect's expectations. You are also responsible for making certain you are able to fulfill these expectations.

Your ability to fulfill your prospect's expectations is important because it will have a direct impact on whether or not this person is satisfied. Customer satisfaction is a topic I will explore in Chapter Eleven of this book when I introduce a program for "managing satisfaction." For now, I shall introduce this concept for two reasons. First, the notion of a satisfied customer relates to your overall sales and marketing effort. Second, this concept underscores the point I made at the outset of this chapter; namely that <u>selling is only one part of your overall business</u>.

To illustrate this point, when I was younger, I had the opportunity to work for a publishing company. My job was to handle all telephone accounts. These accounts were typically customers and potential customers (i.e. prospects) who were located in geographical regions of the U.S. too costly to visit. Therefore, I developed a telephone solicitation program to persuade these people to purchase one of my company's products.

One of the prospects I contacted was a large distributor. Since he represented a sizeable account, I was instructed to "take no prisoners" and get his business. I knew of an exciting new product the firm had recently unveiled. I believed this product would be compatible with my prospect's other merchandise and would therefore be a profitable addition to his business. I was able to persuade him that he needed my product because of its ability to meet his business needs. Unfortunately, after I made the sale, I discovered that the item in question could not be produced for at least another year. In their enthusiasm to unveil this exciting new product, my superiors had omitted this small detail. Needless to say, I lost the account.

As a result of this experience, I learned that building credibility is like building a forest. If it is to grow, then it must be continually nurtured. A business relationship, if it is to grow, must also be continually nurtured. The loss of credibility, like a fire in a forest, can destroy everything that you have worked to build. And, while a successful sales strategy can create a "selling opportunity," other elements of the business must be considered prior to the sale because they may determine your success or failure.

KNOWING WHEN TO SAY NO
&
UNDERSTANDING THE FACTORS OF SUCCESS

The aforementioned example is important because it forces you to examine the big picture and ask yourself a very important question, namely, <u>Can my organization meet the needs of my customer</u>? One of the most difficult lessons I learned occurred when I owned my own business. I was responsible for paying all of the bills. I had the opportunity to accept work which might have made the difference between making money and losing money during a given month. Nevertheless, I also understood that, given the limitations of my operation, there were certain types of jobs which I could not do. What was at issue was not my ability to produce the work, but my ability to meet a particular customer's exact specifications. To have taken a particular job and failed to meet a customer's requirements for that job would have meant failing to satisfy that customer. A disatisfied customer would not only refuse to do business with me again, but might discourage other customers from doing business with me as well. Therefore, like Nancy Reagan, I learned the importance of "Just Say No" when it came to disappointing my customers by failing to meet their expectations. If I was unable to do the job, I was usually given the opportunity to bid on other work. If, however, I made a promise I could not keep, I was never given a second chance.

Looking at the big picture means understanding the factors of success which influence your organization. In analyzing my business, I discovered five factors of success or five functions which I needed to properly perform if I were to be successful and achieve my desired objectives. My five factors of success were:

1. PRODUCING QUALITY WORK

Quality sells! It is important for the Owner, or someone in the company, to be responsible for reviewing the quality of the work produced. The litmus test is to ask yourself one very important question: "Would I pay money for this?" If the answer is no then do it over and do it right. Be honest with yourself and do not be afraid to bring the boss the bad news. If you know there is a problem, then the boss will be indebted to you for bringing it to his attention. He may have suspected something wasn't right and be grateful that there is someone in his organization who is looking out for his best interest. If, one the other hand, his response is one of anger and hostility, then it is obvious that he is part of the problem and it is time for you to look for greener pastures. Remember, it is better to be the first mate on the Good Ship Lollypop than the captain of the Titanic.

2. PROVIDING GOOD SERVICE

Remember, the customer pays the bills! If you own your own business then you understand this simple fact. If not, then it is important to remember that even the "Top Dog" has a master who puts the food in his dish. It is extremely important for you to make every effort to fulfill your customer's expectations and treat him or her with concern. I will never forget the story of a wealthy alumnus who was going to make a multimillion dollar contribution to his alma mater. He changed his mind at the last minute because he was greeted by a rude receptionist who didn't care about him or his money.

The litmus test for providing good service is to treat your customer in the same manner you would want to be treated. The best formula for standing apart from your competition is to let your customers know that you care. It is also the foundation for repeat business. If, as I have often heard stated, courtesy is contagious, then it should be your job to spread this disease. [In Chapter Eleven, I will outline a system for monitoring customer satisfaction and making certain that all of your customers are happy customers].

3. DEVELOPING A CONSISTENT MARKETING PROGRAM

I will explore this theme in greater detail in Chapters Four through Eight. I shall introduce it at this time, however, as one of the five factors of success. Be persistent and consistent! In the battle for the hearts and minds of customers, it is very important to send a message and reinforce that message. Use multiple marketing media. Develop a message which allows you to offer your potential customers something their competitors do not offer them. [Advertisers refer to this concept as the "Unique Selling Proposition" and I will discuss it in greater detail in Chapter Three].

4. MANAGING YOUR EXPENSES

Carefully monitor your expenses! Control your costs of production, make certain your pricing system is enabling you to achieve an adequate return on your investment, maintain an inventory turnover which is appropriate and in accordance with your industry, and develop a receivables policy that makes sense for your business!

I do not plan to elaborate on managing expenses because it is not the purpose of this book. Nevertheless, you should realize that your organization may have the most effective marketing program in the world and still fail if expenses are not properly controlled. Contrary to popular belief, you cannot raise your prices to cover the cost of your mistakes and remain competitive. While some people are willing to pay more money for better quality and service, they are not willing to pay more money to subsidize incompetent management.

If managing expenses is not a part of your job, it still doesn't hurt to ask intelligent questions. By doing so, you learn things which enable you to do your job better. You also demonstrate to those who are in a position to promote you that you are worth promoting.

5. BELIEVING IN YOURSELF

Never lose faith! One important rule of business is that people like to do business with a winner. No one is immune from failure and catastrophe. But failure and catastrophe, unlike courtesy, is something others do not want to be a part of--they would rather avoid you than be made uneasy by your self doubt. If you encounter someone who likes to discuss failure then avoid this person. Otherwise, you may find yourself falling victim to his dark outlook.

Never share you failures with anyone except your closest confidants! Select confidants who are not associated with your company or profession. The person or persons whom you occasionally reveal your doubts or failures to should be people who are willing to listen and offer their support. Do not confide in anyone who will use your information to pass judgement on your worth as a human being or use privileged information to advance themselves at your expense. Be careful.

Above all, remember that in sales, as in roulette, failure has no memory. Just because one prospect gave you an icy reception doesn't mean the next person is not ready to eat out of your hand. Just make certain you do not carry the memory of that frigid prospect with you to your next encounter.

THE ACTION PLAN

The five factors of success I have outlined may also apply to your organization. I recommend that you make a list of those factors you believe determine whether or not your business is achieving its desired objectives. You may decide to use my list as a starting point. If I have cited something which you consider to be inappropriate then delete it from your list. If I have omitted something which you consider to be appropriate then add it to your list. But take the time to list the success factors influencing your business because, before we can explore specific strategies and techniques you will want to consider in your common sense sales approach, we will use these factors to develop an <u>action plan</u>.

An action plan involves an effort to translate the factors you consider important to the success of your organization into actions which can be implemented by you or others. This plan is a statement of how you will achieve your success goals. Since our objective is to focus on selling, we will examine the success factors relating to our ability to sell. The action plan is important because it will serve as a guide which enables you to assemble a marketing program that meets the needs of your business or profession. Without an understanding of what those needs are and how they can best be served, devising an appropriate common sense sales strategy is difficult. I have outlined a sample action plan for the fictitious XYZ Company.

THE XYZ COMPANY
ACTION PLAN FOR THE ACHIEVEMENT OF SUCCESS OBJECTIVES
The five variables necessary to achieve XYZ's success objectives are:

1. <u>QUALITY</u>-All work must adhere to the highest standards of quality. It is the responsibility of Randolph Smith, V.P. for Quality Assurance, to supervise production and make certain that the quality of the end-product is satisfactory. If there are any questions or problems, R. Smith will contact the appropriate individual(s) (i.e. sales, production, accounting). R. Smith will also review the work order to make certain that all customer requirements are being met. Any customer inquiries will be referred to R. Smith.

2. <u>TIMELINESS</u>-Every effort will be made to produce work in a timely manner. The time constraints imposed by the customer will be honored whenever possible. The exception to this rule concerns any action or actions that would

compromise the quality of the work being produced. James Newhouse, Production Manager, will be responsible for scheduling work and meeting all production deadlines.

     3. <u>COMPETITOR ANALYSIS</u>-Five to six competitors will be targeted each quarter for a review of performance. Betty Williamson, Customer Service Manager, will be responsible for contacting these businesses. The competitors chosen will be businesses that do quality work and adhere to professional standards similar to those of XYZ. B. Williamson will determine whether or not XYZ is offering products of similar quality and comparable price. She will also compile a report on competitive strengths and weaknesses in the area of service delivery. This report will be distributed to all employees and a quarterly meeting will be held to discuss its findings.

     4. <u>CUSTOMER CARE</u>-Each and every customer will be made to feel that his business is important. The customer follow-up program will be strictly adhered to. Linda Daniels, Assistant Customer Service Manager, will be in charge of program implementation and compliance. Any questions regarding this program should be directed to her.

     5. <u>PROMOTION</u>-The quality, timeliness, dependability, and customer concern will be communicated to all customers as part of our advertising program. This program will serve to distinguish XYZ from its competition. Bill Stevens, Advertising Manager, will supervise the program. He will also be available to answer any questions and provide other employees with information regarding how they can use XYZ's advertising program to emphasize the positive features of our company.

     The aforementioned action plan addresses the sales and marketing goals which affect, either directly or indirectly, our fictitious company. XYZ has defined its factors of success. Their action plan represents a blueprint for achieving these objectives.

     Each objective is stated in a format which instructs employees on how it is to be implemented. Individuals are assigned the responsibility for determining that the objectives of the plan are being achieved. By placing employees in charge, worker involvement and participation is enhanced. Common sense dictates that, if the organization is to achieve its success goals, then all of its members must understand what these goals are and how they can participate in achieving them. Our sample action plan is geared to achieve this task. It also provides direction for the actual sales and marketing campaign by providing a veritable "treasure chest" of selling benefits which can be communicated to prospective customers.

Action plans, like XYZ's, are not meant to intimidate. These plans are easier to develop than you might realize. Developing the plan simply involves taking the time to decide what will need to be done and who will need to do it. Critics of this type of planning contend that, given the incessant demands on one's time in the "real world," long-range planning is impractical. I would argue that the failure to develop goals and a game plan to achieve those goals is tantamount to sailing a ship without a rudder. While a rudderless vessel may move fast, it seldom goes where one wants it to go. If you are to achieve your professional objectives, then you will need a plan for attaining these objectives.

An action plan can be developed for organizations of any size or scope. If you operate your own business and are the sole employee, then developing the plan means taking the time to organize your responsibilities into manageable components. In a single person operation, there are no lines of responsibility. Nevertheless, it is important to have a clear understanding of your responsibilities. An action plan can provide you with such an understanding.

If your organization includes more than one person, your plan provides the advantage of clarifying lines of responsibility within the organization. If you are not the leader of the pack—but wish to advance—presenting this plan to one of your superiors could give you the career boost you desire. I suggest that you present your plan at a meeting focusing on ways to improve efficiency and productivity within your organization. Such a meeting would provide you with the ideal forum to demonstrate that you are a "shining star" and possess the potential to do great things. From my own experience as the owner of a small company, I know how difficult it is to recruit and retain good personnel. An employee who demonstrates his intelligence and productivity is an employee to be rewarded--or lost!

Three important features emerge from the action plan. First, it provides the organization with a direction for its common sense sales campaign. It does this by detailing how the company plans to achieve its desired objectives. Second, the plan enhances employee participation and involvement, thereby increasing the likelihood that all employees will pursue its objectives. It does this by establishing clear lines of authority and assigning certain individuals specific areas of responsibility. Third, the plan provides a concrete set of selling benefits. These benefits provide a powerful incentive to attract potential customers. In order to attract these customers, however, these benefits must be effectively communicated. By doing so, we create a "selling opportunity." But before we can create this opportunity, it is important to understand the process of selling. It is this process that we shall now examine.

3 What is selling?

Earlier, we defined selling as the ability to persuade your prospect that he or she needs your product or service based on its ability to fill a perceived need or set of needs. Selling involves understanding the needs of your prospect and being able to relate those needs to your product or service. [For purposes of clarity, I shall henceforth use the term "product" to refer both to products and services.] You listen and, based on what you are told, establish a need in the mind of your prospect. By creating a need and demonstrating how your product can fill this need, you create an expectation. It is this expectation, however, which must be managed.

What do I mean by "managing your prospect's expectations?" What I mean is that you create a promise that must be fulfilled or else you will lose your customer. In the last chapter, I stated three important features which emerge from your action plan. I shall now cite a fourth feature. It is an understanding of the limitations of your organization. This understanding of limitations is known as knowing when to say no. Nonetheless, in sales, you never want to say no. These two statements appear contradictory. In reality, they are not. Allow me to explain.

In his book entitled *Going For It*, Victor ("Close as a blade or your money back") Kiam describes selling as the ability to paint a vista on a broad canvas. The vista you paint is a vision of your prospect entering the promised land. This promised land may involve more money, fewer hassles, faster turnaround time or any other benefit you perceive as being important to your prospect. Remember, you are not selling a product. You are selling the solution to a problem. Therefore, your challenge is to take what you have to offer and tailor it to meet your customer's needs. I shall illustrate.

Assume Tom Tuttle is a salesperson for the XYZ Company. Tom has reviewed his action plan and has determined that XYZ's principal strengths (i.e., selling benefits) versus its competition are: 1) faster turnaround time and 2) a guarantee of product quality. Now let's devise a meeting between Tom and Larry Foster, Vice-President of Distribution for the ABC Company. In our first scenario, Tom fails to match his selling strengths with the needs of his prospect. The meeting unfolds as follows:

SCENARIO ONE

Tom: "Larry, I appreciate the opportunity to meet with you today and determine if our product can meet your needs."

Larry: "Look Tom, I'll get right to the point. The president of our company has informed me that we have to reduce costs. Therefore, my primary goal is to reduce product costs. I'm looking at the cheapest price I can get. DEF Company can produce widgets for us at a price per thousand of $1,200. Can you beat that price?"

[Please note that a widget is a fictitious product]

Tom: "No Larry, I can't, but let me tell you what I can offer you..."

Don't bother, Tom. In our first scenario, Larry Foster was kind enough to tell Tom Tuttle that his most important concern regarded product cost. Sometimes, you have to ask many questions before discovering your prospect's "hot button." I define "hot button" as the issue or issues of greatest concern. Unfortunately, Tom was unable to match his selling strengths or product benefits with Larry's major concern. By telling Larry that he could not compete with DEF Company solely on the basis of the lowest price per thousand, Tom forfeited an opportunity to sell Larry his product. Imagine a situation in which you discover that you have a termite infestation in your home or apartment. No sooner do you make this discovery than there is a knock at the door. An individual introduces himself to you as an exterminator of household pets. Your first question will obviously be "Can you kill termites?" If he says, "No, but let me tell you about all of the other household pets I can kill," your response will be, "Thanks, but no thanks."

I have decided, however, to give Tom a second chance to make a first impression. In our second scenario, Tom does match his selling benefits with his customer's needs as follows:

SCENARIO TWO

Tom: "Larry, I appreciate the opportunity to meet with you today and determine whether our product can meet your needs."

Larry: "Look Tom, I'll get right to the point. The president of our company has informed me that we have to reduce costs. Therefore, my primary goal is to reduce product costs. I'm looking at the cheapest price I can get. DEF Company can produce widgets for us at a price per thousand of $1,200. Can you beat that price?"

Tom: "Larry, if I understand you correctly, product cost is your most important consideration and your decision regarding which company you will choose is based on the cost of the product to the company. Is that correct?"

Larry: "That's it in a nutshell, Tom."

Tom: "Well Larry, let me ask you another question regarding product cost. Are you currently satisfied with the turnaround time you are getting and the quality of the product you are receiving?"

Larry: "Tom, now that you mention it, I have been concerned with turnaround time. Our current supplier is getting slower and slower. And the quality of the product is not what it used to be."

Tom: "Larry, do you feel that a slower turnaround time and deteriorating product quality could also be increasing your costs of doing business?"

Larry: "As a matter of fact, I do."

Tom: "If I could offer you a product that is competitively priced, could be delivered on time, and has a guarantee of superior quality, would you be interested?"

Larry: "That sounds like the answer to my problem!"

In our second scenario, Tom listened to Larry's concerns and demonstrated that he understood those concerns. After Larry initially challenged Tom to "beat the price," Tom had essentially three options. First, he could have ignored Larry and begun his prerehearsed sales pitch. This would have probably cost him the sale. Second, he could have (and did in our first scenario) stated he could not match DEF Company's price and then proceed with his product pitch. This would have definitely cost him the sale. Third, Tom could (and did in our second scenario) demonstrate to Larry that product cost involved more than simply a price per thousand. Product cost also involved turnaround time and product quality, which coincidentally happen to be the strengths of Tom's product. Tom demonstrated to Larry that: 1) he was listening to his problem, 2) he was responding to his needs, 3) Larry's concerns regarding cost involved more than simply price and 4) given his redefinition of Larry's problem, Tom had the solution.

REDEFINING THE PROBLEM

The important point in our second example is that Tom was able to <u>redefine</u> Larry's concern without changing his basic problem. Tom knew what the strengths of his product were. After listening to Larry, he understood what his primary concern was. By redefining Larry's problem without changing it, Tom was able to create expectations and manage those expectations. He did this by demonstrating to Larry that turnaround time and product quality (the inherent strengths of Tom's product) were part of Larry's problem. Once Larry accepted this proposition, Tom proceeded to create "manageable expectations" by matching his prospect's concern with his product's benefits.

How does one know if a product has been redefined without being changed? Simply by asking the customer, as Tom did, the following question:

Tom: "Larry, do you feel that a slower turnaround time and deteriorating product quality could also be increasing your costs of doing business?"

Larry: "As a matter of fact, I do."

Tom, in our example, tested his new definition of the problem on Larry and he received a response which indicated he had successfully redefined the problem. Once Tom received an affirmative response, he was able to give Larry the good news. Tom had the solution to Larry's redefined problem! More importantly, Tom was able to avoid the pitfalls of having to say no or of misrepresenting XYZ's product. Tom created a win-win situation, which is the most favorable type of situation in selling.

What if Larry had given Tom a negative response? Then, Tom's next move would have been to attempt another redefinition of the problem. This redefinition, however, would still need to be compatible with the benefits Tom's product could offer. "Redefining the problem" does not always result in a sale. No sales approach, regardless of the fantastic claims made by its creator, results in a sale one-hundred percent of the time. The reality of our situation, however, is that Tom cannot sell Larry widgets at a price per thousand of $1,200. If Tom accepts this as the make or break condition, then he will fail to get the sale. If, however, he redefines the problem by relating it to something he can offer Larry, then he has an opportunity to sell Larry his widgets. <u>Selling involves creating opportunities.</u> <u>The more opportunities you create to sell your products, the more sales you will</u>

<u>actually make</u>.

THE ANATOMY OF A SALE

From our previous example, certain characteristics emerge which form a necessary part of a common sense approach to selling. Before we can move to a discussion of specific strategies for building a customer clientele, however, it is important for you to understand these variables. I shall refer to them as "the anatomy of a sale."

I have read numerous book, listened to countless tapes and attended endless seminars on selling. My criticism of these books, tapes and seminars is that they tend to transform selling into something complicated and unnatural. An elaborate program is presented to the participants and it is their responsibility to master this material. I would compare the programs I have studied to attempting to run a fifty yard dash in a maze. One falls short of one's ultimate goal because one becomes preoccupied with the process and loses sight of the goal.

A favorite example of mine involves a personal experience. When I was hired by a fortune 500 firm to serve in their sales and marketing division, I was sent to corporate headquarters to participate in a "training program." The company had spent thousands of dollars to provide its recruits with a comprehensive program designed to teach each of us how to sell. The instructors were men with impressive credentials and they presented the class with an elaborate series of rules and procedures. They told us that if we were to be successful then we would have to master this maze of material.

When our instructors were satisfied that they had properly indoctrinated us with their secrets of successful selling, we were given the opportunity to practice through a process of role playing. I was chosen to play the role of a prospect. A fellow classmate, who had sufficiently impressed our instructors with his mastery of the material, was chosen to play the role of the super salesperson. This salesperson demonstrated his mastery of the material and played his role brilliantly. Unfortunately, there was one small problem. Midway through his presentation, I decided to send a "buy signal" (i.e. indicate a willingness to purchase the product). The super salesperson, however, had not completed the "selling checklist" his instructors had indicated must be completed before a sale could be successfully attempted. Consequently, while I was ready to buy, he was not ready to sell. By the time he was ready to sell, I had lost all interest in the product and therefore dismissed him. My instructors angrily informed me that I had not played my role properly. I did not realize that the people who purchase products are supposed to be trained on how to buy. Unfortunately for my hapless instructors, neither do most customers.

The moral of this story is not to become preoccupied with artificial processes or elaborate procedures. The core of common sense selling is selling which is sensible and comfortable—sensible meaning it is understandable and comfortable meaning the person making the sale can be himself. <u>The litmus test is to ask yourself two very important questions. First, does this sales approach make sense? Second, does it feel comfortable?</u> If you have to follow a step-by-step program that neither feels comfortable nor makes sense then you are in trouble. If, on the other hand, you are presented with a series of tools and can choose those which do feel comfortable and make sense then you are less likely to fail. You are less likely to fail because you are able to be yourself. Remember: any selling strategy that does not allow you to be yourself is likely to make you uncomfortable. And, by being uncomfortable, you will make your prospect uneasy. Uneasiness, like courtesy, is contagious. Unlike courtesy, it is a prescription for disaster. Therefore, if it does not feel comfortable or make sense to you then your prospect probably won't buy it either.

THE RULES OF THE GAME

Hopefully, I have convinced you that if it's complicated and confusing then it's not for you. If, on the other hand, it is comfortable and does make sense then you should be willing to try it. With this fact in mind, I shall unveil my "rules of the game." Once you have created the opportunity to sell your product, these rules are intended to assist you in making the sale.

If these rules appear simplistic, do not panic. Whether or not the tools I offer you in *Common Sense Selling* are new and revolutionary is unimportant. What is important is your ability to use these tools to attract new customers and achieve your desired objectives. If what you read appears familiar, remember: seeing these ideas expressed on paper and discovering new ways you can apply them can make a tremendous difference. Even if you succeed in attracting only one additional customer as a result of an idea or a strategy you discover in this book, you should still realize a return on your investment (i.e., the price you paid for this book) of at least one thousand percent. Any seasoned investor will tell you that a return of one thousand percent on any investment is definitely worth having.

The rules of the game of common sense selling are as follows:

1. **KNOW YOUR PRODUCT**-Before attempting to make a sale, whether it be over the counter or out in the field, know your product. Understand the benefits you have to offer potential customers as well as any weaknesses (i.e., something your competition may be able to offer which you cannot). You should be able to

anticipate likely questions or objections a customer might pose. While you should not become preoccupied with anticipating every possible question or overcoming every possible objection, you should have a "feel" for what it is your customers will want to know or might find objectionable. There is no substitute for knowledge of your product. I have seen men and women rise through the ranks of organizations because they possessed a thorough knowledge of what their company had to offer. These men and women made themselves indispensable. I even know of one individual who had converted a room in his home into a product training center which he used to train himself on every facet of his company's product line. Needless to say, this man did extremely well with his firm and became indispensable to top management whenever they were called upon to discuss and defend their product line.

Remember, to be an effective salesperson, common sense selling dictates that you are able to "connect" with your potential customer. Connecting means being able to establish a rapport with your prospect based on trust and likability. In order to build trust, you must know your product. Never tell a customer something you believe he or she wants to hear if you know it is not true. You might make the sale by doing so, but once your customer discovers that you lied, he is likely to return to the scene of the crime and make life very difficult for you. Unhappy customers are detrimental to your financial health and job security—particularly if your boss happens to be on the premises when your irate customer returns on his search and destroy mission.

One question I have encountered from students of selling is "What do I do if I do not know the answer to a customer's question?" My response is that it is better to risk losing the sale than risk lying to the customer. There is, however, another alternative. One technique I have learned and will share with you is what I refer to as "working on the customer's behalf." This is a technique you will be able to use in certain situations.

Let's assume a customer walks into my business and asks me for a price on a particular job. If I am unable to calculate the price immediately, my response is to tell the customer that, if he would permit me to contact several of my suppliers, I believe I can do better than the standard price. Would the customer, therefore, allow me to take his name, telephone number and contact him after I had spoken to my suppliers? I have never had a customer respond "No, I want the higher price immediately!" Normally, I could not quote the price immediately because the job was of a highly specialized nature. The customer, however, tended to be quite pleased that I was willing to work on his behalf to get him the best possible price. In these situations, I transformed an "I don't know" into an "I'd really like to have your business and am therefore willing to work to get you the best possible price." What is interesting to note is that when I recontacted these customers, they tended to be pleased with whatever price they were quoted because I had created an impression in their minds that I was working on their behalf. Remember, if you can transform an "I don't know" into an "I'd really like to have your business and am therefore willing to work to get you the best possible price," then you build a bond of trust with your customers. And you may discover the amount of work performed is no greater than if you had said, "I don't know." While the amount of work is no greater, your customers good will toward you has increased immeasurably.

2. **KNOW YOUR PROSPECT**-Once you have learned your product, you need to know your prospect. Unfortunately, it is often impossible to do any advance preparation. If would be nice if someone could provide you with a dossier containing all of the relevant information you need to know before confronting each potential customer. Unfortunately, the real world seldom provides you with such luxuries. What is possible, however, is to learn as you go. The way to do this is by <u>listening</u>. Once you have introduced yourself, ask your prospect what he considers to be important in a business which offers what you have to offer. It has been my experience that most people, if given the opportunity, love to talk about themselves and their businesses. In these situations, if you simply give this person the opportunity, he will create that dossier of relevant information which can make all of the difference in the world.

One trap salespeople fall into is an obsession with "losing control." It is their fear that, if they allow their prospects to say two words, then they will have lost control of the sale. What these paranoid people fail to understand is that monopolizing the conversation simply serves to reinforce all of the negative stereotypes (e.g., pushy, overbearing, or rude) individuals have of salespeople. In their misguided efforts to avoid losing control they invariably lose the sale.

Maintaining control simply means setting the agenda. You set an agenda by "steering the conversation" and "moving from weakness to strength." An example of "steering the conversation" would be a situation in which, after you have introduced yourself to your prospect, he proceeds to tell you his life story. It is important for you to interject a comment that will redirect the conversation in the direction you need to pursue—namely a discussion of the prospect's business needs and how your product might fit those needs. Such an comment might be, "Mr. Smith, it's obvious you have led a fascinating life. What particularly interests me is how your business operates and how I might be able to play a small role in such an exciting and successful operation." Or, "I understand your business is undergoing some exciting changes. Perhaps, if I had a better understanding of your current business needs, I might be able to help you."

Either of these comments should enable you to put the conversation on the right track without appearing to the prospect that you are attempting to monopolize the conversation or force the sale. Depending on the nature of your business, the initial contact may be exploratory and it is therefore extremely important for you to learn all that you can. Remember: common sense selling means knowing

20

your product and knowing your customer.

The other agenda setting technique is "moving from weakness to strength." This merely means taking a question or objection and translating it into a positive attribute. A favorite example of mine involves a job interview. In this interview, my job was to sell myself. The interviewer was clever and he asked me the following question: "Mr. Pattiz, you have done a most effective job of listing your strengths, but surely no one is without weaknesses. Please give me one of your weaknesses and indicate why you consider it to be a weakness?" I had no intention of handing the interviewer ammunition which he could use to disqualify me from the position, so I gave the following response: "Well, one weakness is my preoccupation with productivity. Former employers have told me that no sooner do they give me an assignment than I have completed it and am hounding them for more work. On the other hand, this could be interpreted as a strength as well because . . . " I simply outfoxed the interviewer by taking what appeared to be a weakness and quickly transforming it into a strength. Needless to say, I was offered the job.

Prospects, like the interviewer in our example, can challenge you by confronting you with something they perceive as a weakness or you know to be a weakness. Remember Tom Tuttle of XYZ Company. When he was challenged to "beat the price" DEF Company was offering per thousand widgets, Tom confronted a weakness. He knew his company could not compete with DEF solely on the basis of product cost. He therefore introduced timeliness and quality as components of his prospect's cost concern. When this person concurred, Tom succeeded in moving him to an area of XYZ's product strength.

I referred to the importance of building a relationship based on trust and likability. Trust implies understanding the problems confronting your potential customer and being able to help him solve those problems. It is important to view your role as that of a "problem solver" in order to avoid the tendency to jam a square peg into a round hole. This phenomenon occurs when the salesperson tries to meet his needs instead of the needs of his customer. By failing to see the big picture in terms of his prospect's needs, the salesperson may fail to see how he can adapt his product to meet those needs. Instead, he simply attempts to force his prospect to purchase his product. This strategy seldom works.

The other feature of the relationship between buyer and seller is likability. I used to believe this was meaningless until I purchased a business. I competed against people with superior products who failed because customers did not like them and against people with inferior products who succeeded because customers did like them. I am reminded of the story Lee Iacocca told of how he was called into the office of Henry Ford II, to be informed he was being fired despite his remarkable accomplishments. The reason Mr. Ford gave for dismissing Mr. Iacocca was that he did not like him.

Likability is something which I do not believe can be taught.   While you cannot be taught how to be instantly likeable, I do believe you can learn how to "soften" certain personality traits which others may find offensive. My advice in this area is to show your prospect that you genuinely care about him and his business. Listening is one way to do this. I have discovered, however, that personality conflicts will arise for no rational reason. If you believe you have made every effort to satisfy a particular prospect's needs and still sense hostility, my best advice is to walk away. Give someone else the wonderful privilege of doing business with this good natured soul. If, on the other hand, a pattern develops whereby you are consistently experiencing this problem, then it is obvious that you are the problem and it is time for you to make some changes.

Now it is time to introduce my final rule of the game of common sense selling. Unlike many self-proclaimed experts, it is not my intention to dazzle you with elaborate procedures or complicated rules. I believe in the KISS (Keep It Simple, Stupid!) Concept. I also believe in the importance of providing you with ideas and suggestions which make sense and are easy to implement. Remember, if it's complicating and confusing, then it is not for you.

3. **KNOW YOURSELF**-Once you have familiarized yourself with your product and your prospect, it is time to "build a bridge" between what you have and what your prospect needs. In the following chapters, I will outline specific strategies for attracting customers. For now, it is important to review the rules of how to sell your prospect so you do not fall flat on your face once you have created a selling opportunity.

Building a bridge between what you have and what your prospect needs involves knowing, not only your product and your prospect, but yourself as well. No product, no matter how spectacular, can sell itself. If it could, then there would be no need for salespeople. It is the job of the salesperson to sell the potential customer. To be successful, the salesperson needs to understand what he or she has to offer the prospect. Understanding what you have to offer means establishing a rapport with the person you are attempting to sell to. The question remains: What does all of this have to do with selling?

The answer is simple. You are attempting to "connect." Remember, we defined connecting as being able to build a relationship based on trust and likability. To do this, you need to know what you and your prospect have in common. By knowing yourself, you can also determine what it is about you that might make your prospect uneasy.

One method for getting to know yourself better is to make a list of what you perceive as your strengths and weaknesses. Such a list might be as follows:

ANALYSIS OF STRENGTHS & WEAKNESSES

STRENGTHS	WEAKNESSES
Honest	Abrasive
Straightforward	Short-Tempered
Thorough	Obsessed With Details
Loyal	Tend To Form Personal Biases
Hard-Working	Tendency To Overwork
Enthusiastic	Naive
Insightful	Too Introspective
Gregarious	Tendency To Talk Too Much

In this example, every strength I cite has a corresponding weakness. You should attempt to determine whether each of your strengths might have a corresponding weakness. Once you have completed your list, ask three people who know you to make a list of what they perceive to be your strengths and weaknesses. Select three people whom you know in different capacities (e.g. spouse, co-worker, friend). Compare the lists and look for common areas of agreement. Do not be surprised if their lists contain strengths and weaknesses which do not appear on your list. It is important for you to understand how others see you.

Once you have analyzed your strengths and weaknesses, go one step further. Compile a list of things you like and dislike. Such a list might appear as follows:

ANALYSIS OF LIKES & DISLIKES

LIKES	DISLIKES
Golf	Cooking
Classical Music	Shopping
Reading—Especially Novels	Rock Music
Movies—Particularly Westerns	Politics
Swimming	Hot Weather
Camping	Working Late
Traveling	Gardening
Old Coins	Loud Noises

The purpose of this exercise and the previous exercise is to learn as much about yourself as you possibly can. This is to assist you in making the sale. You may already believe you know all there is to know, but compile your list anyway because you may learn something about yourself you did not know. And what you learn may make the difference in terms of getting the sale. The question remains: How will any of this help me?

To answer this question, I shall introduce a concept I call "Commonalities." What this means is making yourself more like your customer. In order to make yourself more like your customer, you need to know what area or areas you may have in common. This concept does not mean adopting similar behavior patterns as those of your customers (i.e., if he talks slow then you talk slow). The problem with that approach is that it could violate our basic rule of being ourselves.

What I refer to by "commonalities" is making a determination that you and your prospect may share a particular interest or possess a similar personality trait. By knowing this, you can establish likability. Let's assume you know your prospect likes classical music and you like classical music. Introduce this topic into your conversation. Remember, one of the most powerful characteristics of human nature is that people like to do business with people who are like themselves. Your prospect may be searching for some common ground to determine whether or not you are someone he feels comfortable doing business with. Your job is to help him find this common ground.

A word of warning. Do not fall into the trap of attempting to build a relationship based on false interests. If you know your prospect likes classical music, but you do not know the first thing about classical music, don't try to impress him by saying, "Yeah, that Beethoven, he's a swell guy. You know, I've got his greatest hits album." If your prospect senses your insincerity, he will begin to doubt your ability to serve his professional needs. Do not bluff. If you do, you may be "hung out to dry."

As the owner of a small company, I belonged to the local area chamber of commerce. I attended many functions sponsored by the chamber and observed how the concept of "commonalities" enabled people to do business with one another. Remember, a prospect who senses that you share his interests is more likely to believe that you understand his problems. [In Chapter Ten, I will demonstrate how you can catalogue important facts about areas of common interest thereby enabling you to reactivate the feelings of friendship and goodwill each time you contact your customers.]

SUMMARY

In Chapters Two and Three, we examined several important concepts. By determining the success factors which influence your organization and developing an action plan that describes how these factors are to be achieved, you can develop your professional game plan. This game plan specifies your goals, the means of achieving those goals, and what strengths (selling benefits) you possess to assist you in achieving those goals. I also discussed the importance of creating expectations which are manageable. To do this, you may need to "redefine" your prospect's concerns without changing those concerns.

We reviewed the"rules of the game" of common sense selling. Those rules are:

KNOW YOUR PRODUCT
KNOW YOUR PROSPECT
KNOW YOURSELF

Once you have created the opportunity to sell your product, these rules are intended to assist you in making the sale. These rules are your tools. Use them to sell to your customers and build relationships with people who will want to do business with you again and again and again.

I introduced the concept of "setting the agenda" through the process of "steering the conversation" and "moving from weakness to strength." In this discussion, the importance of building a relationship based on trust and likability was stressed. Finally, the concept of "commonalities" was introduced as a reason for learning as much as you can about yourself.

I hope that you now have a better understanding of how to sell to your prospect. It is important to know how to sell before you can attempt to create a selling opportunity. Otherwise, you might discover that once you have your prospect's attention, you do not know how to transform his interest into a sale.

Unfortunately, some companies spend millions of dollars on advertising, which is intended to attract customers, only to belatedly discover that their sales force lacks the skills needed to "build a bridge" between what they have to offer and what their customers need to have. These companies put the Cart before the Ox by sending their armies onto the beaches of opportunity without equipping them with the necessary tools to do the job.

A battleplan for capturing the hearts and minds of customers.

In chapter two, I stated that, in the battle for the hearts and minds of customers, it is very important to send a message and reinforce that message. This point needs to be stressed. If your goal is to attract customers then your marketing strategy must be clear and consistent. Common sense selling dictates that you be persistent and consistent in your approach. You are attempting to occupy a place in the mind of your prospect. In the case of Tom Tuttle and XYZ, it was Tom's job to make certain that when a prospect thought of widgets, XYZ popped into his mind. America's most successful companies have based their advertising strategies on their ability to get people to think of them when they think of their products. Their goal is to make themselves synonymous with whatever it is they offer.

In devising your common sense sales campaign, your goal should be to make yourself synonymous with whatever it is that you offer. When the prospect thinks of your product, he should be thinking of you.

ANALYZING THE MARKET & THE COMPETITION

The battleplan you develop to capture the hearts and minds of your customers must be based on your understanding of the marketplace. The first step is to identify the heavy users of your product. I define the heavy users as those individuals or organizations who use your product in significant quantities and with sufficient regularity to enable you to achieve your desired objectives. In other words, these are the folks who put the food on your table.

Who are these people and where are they located? You need to know because your advertising strategy will be designed to capture them. There are companies that conduct market analyses and are able to segment any market based on any criteria (e.g., income, education). The local area chamber of commerce may also be able to provide you with this information. Or, you can travel your market and ask people questions. The important point is: <u>You need to focus your attention on the right audience. Common sense selling dictates that you pursue the people who have the greatest need for your product.</u>

It is not my intention to review the ABC's of doing a market analysis because each market is different. My goal is to outline strategies you can use in any marketplace. Nonetheless, it is important for you to take the time to get to know your marketplace or else you will not know where and to whom you should be directing your common sense sales campaign.

Once you have identified the heavy users in your market, how do you interest them in what you have to offer? First, you find out what your competition has to offer. You do this by conducting a "competitor analysis." This is merely a fancy term for shopping your competition. Assume you are the user of your product and develop a list of questions that you would ask someone who provides this type of product. Based on my experience, your list will probably be more extensive than that of an actual user because you have followed my first rule of selling: Know Thy Product.

Once you have compiled your list, start making phone calls. Find out what your competition has to offer and where they fall short. Make certain your questions address the important areas (e.g., product quality, service reliability and price). Take good notes as your competitors answer these questions because you will want to carefully review your findings after you have finished questioning your competition. Your competitor analysis will enable you to compare what you have to offer with what your competition has to offer. If there are any serious deficiencies, which could place you in a vulnerable position, it is important to find out what they are before you commit yourself to a comprehensive sales program. I knew of one case in which an individual discovered that his prices were significantly higher than his competition. After investigating further, he discovered that he was being cheated by his primary supplier. This person changed suppliers and was able to offer competitive prices. Fortunately, he realized this before his customers did. Otherwise, he might have been accused of cheating them!

After reviewing the strengths and weaknesses of your competition, it is time to brainstorm. Your goal in this exercise is to determine: 1) Is there something I am offering that the majority of my competitors are not? 2) Is there a real or perceived weakness on the part of my competition that I can exploit? 3) Can I array my strengths in such a manner as to differentiate myself from my competition? Your findings will lead you to the third step: Developing the "Unique Selling Proposition."

XYZ COMPANY REVISITED
&
THE UNIQUE SELLING PROPOSITION

The third step in developing your battleplan is to develop an advertising approach based on the results of your brainstorming session. To illustrate this concept, we shall use the familiar example of XYZ. Let's assume the company has just opened an office in Boise, Idaho. Tom Tuttle, our intrepid sales sleuth, has been placed in charge of this office. Tom's number one priority is to build customer awareness (i.e., who is XYZ and what do they have to offer?).

Let's also assume XYZ's major product is the self-calibrating widget—a fictitious device used by businesses and individuals. Tom's company has done its homework and provided him with a thorough analysis of the marketplace. This analysis has identified the heavy users. Tom has been provided with a list containing the names, addresses, and telephone numbers of these users.

While Tom's company has provided him with the names of his heavy users, he still has one problem. His company has no name recognition—no one has ever heard of XYZ in Boise. His job, therefore, is similar to the job of someone starting a new business.

Tom has conducted his "competitor analysis" and he has discovered the following: First, the price of XYZ's self-calibrating widget is comparable with the prices of his major competitors. Second, there is no significant difference in quality between XYZ's product and that of the competition. Third, all of the companies Tom contacted stated that, while there is no formal warranty beyond the ninety-day period for parts and labor, they would honor any product problems for up to one year. While this has been stated, <u>these suppliers indicated that they would not put this offer in writing in the form of a guarantee or a warranty</u>.

Tom senses an opportunity. While he perceives no difference between himself and his competitors in the areas of price or quality, it is in the area of service that he senses an advantage. His company offers a standard one-year warranty and an optional three-year warranty. If Tom can use his sales and marketing campaign to stress the fact that XYZ offers a longer warranty on its self-calibrating widgets than any other supplier in the Boise market, then he can distinguish himself from his competition.

Creating a differential advantage (i.e., standing apart from your competition) is what advertisers refer to as the "Unique Selling Proposition." It implies offering your prospects something they are not currently getting anywhere else. Why is this so important?

The reason is obvious. If your goal is to grow then you must appeal to the heavy users. These are people who are currently doing business with someone else. If they are currently doing business with someone else then the question becomes: Why should they do business with you? The Unique Selling Proposition (USP) gives you the opportunity to answer this question. They should be doing business with you because you are offering them something they are not getting from their current supplier.

The question then becomes: Is what you have to offer them, that they are not currently getting, worth having? Or, in our example, do the benefits of doing business with XYZ and receiving a one-year warranty outweigh the costs of ceasing to do business with someone else? This is the challenge Tom must confront if he is to successfully implement his common sense sales program.

WHAT IS IT I AM REALLY OFFERING

When an individual or business enters a new market, it is not unusual to adopt an initial marketing strategy which offers potential customers an incentive to try the new kid on the block. In my case, when I started my business, I distributed coupons as part of a direct sales program to other businesses. These coupons provided a significant cash savings on the purchase of certain products. My decision to offer a coupon was based on my analysis of both the heavy users and the competition. What I discovered was that my market was price sensitive. Therefore, a cash savings program provided a strong incentive.

I went one step farther, however, in creating my USP. Since I understood that the cash savings program I was offering was only intended as a short-term inducement, I also had to assume that people would only do business with me so long as this inducement was offered. They would cease to do business with me unless I offered them with a long-term inducement to continue doing business with me. Therefore, I had to develop a long-term USP which I could stress in my advertising. Like Tom Tuttle, I discovered that my best opportunity to make inroads into the market was in the area of service. I learned from my competitor analysis that the three most common service attributes offered by my competition were: 1) a guarantee of product quality, 2) free pick-up and delivery and 3) convenient credit terms for approved customers.

After reviewing the notes I had taken from my competitor analysis, I realized that, while most competitors offered one or possibly two of these services, none offered all three. Had I made a startling discovery? A word of caution—assuming you discover what appears to be a potential advantage—before you commit yourself in your advertising make certain that the costs of your discovery do not outweigh the benefits. In other words, make sure you can afford to offer what you plan to offer and still realize a reasonable profit from your efforts.

In my case, I could offer all three benefits without adversely affecting my long-term profitability. Therefore, I decided to develop a common sense sales campaign based on these benefits. Earlier, I asked you three very important questions: <u>1) Is there something you are offering that the majority of your competitors are not offering? 2) Is there a real or perceived weakness on the part</u>

of your competition which you can exploit? Or, 3) Can you array your strengths in such a manner as to differentiate yourself from your competition? In this example, I was not offering any single benefit which an interested customer could not have received from one of my competitors. My strategy was to array my strengths in such a manner as to differentiate myself from my competition.

One additional point needs to be made about this strategy. Once you have decided what product strengths or benefits you plan to offer as part of your USP, you need to ask yourself a very important question. What is it I am really offering? In my case, I was not offering: 1) a guarantee of product quality, 2) free pick-up and delivery and 3) convenient credit terms for approved customers. What I was really offering was far more basic: Dependability and Convenience. I was guaranteeing the reliability of my products in order to assure my customers that I was a dependable supplier. I was also making it easy (e.g., free pick-up and delivery) for them to do business with me by stressing convenience.

In an earlier chapter, I discussed the dangers of thinking in narrow terms and failing to grasp opportunities to adapt your product to the changing needs of your marketplace. I am reminded of the story of a man who owned stock in a trolley car company. This man believed the trolley car would fulfill the future transportation needs of a growing America. When he died, he stipulated in his will that his heirs could not sell his stock in the trolley car company for at least ten years. The stock became worthless and his heirs died penniless. The moral of this story is that the man accurately foresaw the need for mass transportation, but he defined this need too narrowly. If he had stipulated that his heirs must invest in some form of mass transportation then he would have given them the flexibility to respond to changes in their environment.

By defining what I was offering my customers in terms of dependability and convenience, I gave myself the flexibility to respond to changes in my environment. And, I discovered a fourth feature related to customer convenience. This fourth benefit involved keeping samples of my customer's work on file. There would be a small additional cost in terms of space requirements, but I estimated that this cost would be more than offset by fewer required pick-ups. I would not have discovered this fourth benefit, however, if I had not asked myself the question: What is it I am really offering?

Phase I of the battleplan for capturing the hearts and minds of your customers involves analyzing your marketplace in terms of: 1) Who are the heavy users of your product(s) and 2) What are the strengths and weaknesses of your competition. Phase II involves using this information to create a "Unique Selling Proposition" (USP) which enables you to distinguish yourself from your competition. Phase III involves taking what you have learned in Phases I & II and "putting it all together" in the form of a common sense sales campaign. Whatever campaign you devise, remember that you will need to periodically review its effectiveness. I suggest that you reevaluate your sales program every six months to determine: 1) if you are achieving your desired objectives and 2) what adjustments you will need to make based on changes in your marketplace.

We move from an understanding of selling and an awareness of your business environment to the mechanics of the sales campaign. For purposes of this book, I will assume your financial resources are limited. Therefore, a multimillion dollar television and radio campaign is not a realistic option. If, however, you are affiliated with an organization that utilizes television or radio, then you will be able to employ what I recommend in conjunction with the electronic sales medium.

I will focus on three distinct sales mediums. I will examine each separately and then outline a comprehensive strategy which utilizes all three. As I mentioned earlier, this book is written for anyone who is interested in selling a product or a service. You may decide that a particular strategy fits your needs or you may decide to employ a more comprehensive approach; such as the one I present in Chapter Eight. Your success or failure does not depend on whether you choose to use every idea or only one. What is important is that you adapt these strategies and suggestions to fit your individual abilities and business requirements. Remember, the litmus test is to ask yourself two questions: <u>First, does this sales approach make sense for me? Second, does it feel comfortable? The essence of common sense selling is selling that is sensible and comfortable.</u>

In the next three chapters, we shall explore three different sales mediums. In Chapter Eight, we will return to the battleplan for capturing the hearts and minds of your customers. I will unveil Phase III of common sense selling—the sales campaign. Using the familiar example of XYZ, I will outline their common sense sales campaign for the Boise market. In Chapter Nine, we will examine how they evaluated the success of this campaign. But let's not get ahead of ourselves. It is now time to introduce the first sales strategy for cultivating new business: **Direct Sales.**

5 **A direct sales program that works.**

For our purposes, I will define direct sales as selling directly to the prospect. This type of common sense selling strategy involves a face-to-face encounter. Typically, during such an encounter, the seller attempts to convince the buyer that he needs the seller's product because of its ability to satisfy the buyer's perceived need or set of needs. In Chapter Three, I described the "rules of the game" of common sense selling. Before a seller can apply these rules, however, he must create an interest in his product. The buyer must be willing to consider whatever it is the seller has to offer. A direct sales program is one means of creating such an interest.

"I CAN'T DO IT!"

At this point, I shall temporarily digress from the topic of direct sales to address a question or a concern which you may have regarding selling. By now, you may have said to yourself: "Okay, Mr. Pattiz, you say that if it isn't making sense or doesn't feel comfortable then don't do it. Well, I don't feel comfortable trying to persuade someone to buy something that he may or may not need." This fear usually arises when I describe someone actually entering an individual's home or place of business in an effort to sell him something.

Each of us, whether we realize it or not, is in the business of selling. In our professional and personal lives, we are constantly challenged to convince and persuade others. As teenagers, we had to sell our parents on the idea that we were responsible and mature enough to drive dad's car or spend the weekend with friends.

I would argue, whether you realize it or not, that you have been selling all your life. Sometimes you succeeded and sometimes you failed, but I doubt that you ever quit. When your parents, spouse or employer rejected one of your ideas or proposals, did you say to yourself, "That's it! I'll never try to sell him on another one of my ideas again!" I think not. In the immortal words of Ginger Rogers, you simply "picked yourself up, dusted yourself off and started all over again."

I have had to train people to sell. In the process, I have encountered the fear which usually arises when an individual visualizes a situation in which I hand him the product and say, "Go in there and sell that old lady a widget or else you're fired!" His fear is one of rejection. People do not like to hear the word 'NO' because they interpret it to mean that they are not good enough. Unfortunately, when some people attempt to sell, they equate failure with the following:

It's not the product; it's not the service; it's certainly not the customer because the customer is an omnipotent being capable of rendering the final judgement on my worth as a human being. Therefore, it must be me. I knew I couldn't do this! I just knew it!

YOU CAN DO IT! BUT IT REALLY DOESN'T MATTER BECAUSE YOU'RE NOT MAKING A SALE, YOU'RE MAKING A FRIEND

If you are reading this book, then I will assume you are someone who is interested in selling. I will also assume, if you are someone who is interested in selling, then you are someone who likes to be liked by other people. Most people like to be liked by other people. If this is the case, then I have just solved your problem. You do not have to do any selling. All you have to do is make friends. That's all!

Before you question my sanity, allow me to explain. Let me begin by assuring you that I am really no different than you. The fears I have cited are legitimate fears which most people experience. Nevertheless, I'll wager you never experienced any fear or anxiety when you gave someone a gift--unless, of course, it was an engagement ring. Therefore, you should experience no fear or anxiety when I present my direct sales program to you because you're really not making a sale: you're making a friend.

Allow me to illustrate. While many people dreaded making sales calls, I always enjoyed them. I enjoyed them because I made them fun. One sales prospecting program I conducted was to canvass the heavy users in my market-area. When I reached the office of the decisionmaker, I was greeted either by him or her—if I was fortunate. Or by his or her secretary—the dreaded gatekeeper—if I was not so fortunate. The conversation went as follows:

Dreaded Gatekeeper: "Can I help you, sir?"

Yours Truly: "No ma'am, actually I stopped by today because I wanted to help you."

Dreaded Gatekeeper: "What!"

Yours Truly: "I wanted to give you this voucher for one hundred dollars."
          [I proceeded to hand her what resembled a check]

Dreaded Gatekeeper: "What!"

Yours Truly: "I know how busy you are and I don't want to take another minute of your time. Thank you so much and have a nice day."

Dreaded Gatekeeper: "Wait! Don't go away! What's this all about?"

Did you ever think that someone would actually be pleading with you to tell them about your product? Probably not. But that's exactly the type of response I encountered. Figure One is a sample voucher.

FIGURE ONE

```
                          XYZ COMPANY
                         3224 Maple Lane
                        Boise, Idaho 30232
                         (xxx) xxx-xxxx

   THIS VOUCHER IS GOOD FOR  $100.00  IN DISCOUNTS


   PAY TO THE ORDER OF_____

                        Bearer must present this voucher with purchase


   EXP. DATE X/X/90        _____
                                        Signature

   This is a non-negotiable item
```

Not only did I have fun making friends, but I made some sales as well. My sales approach has always focused on the "soft sell." I define soft selling as attempting to disarm the prospect through friendly and non-intimidating actions. I transformed the sales call into a "friendship" call and had fun. More importantly, many of my prospects had fun as well. After launching this program, on the very first day, my Customer Service Manager said to me, "You have a ton of messages from people who said that you stopped by earlier in the day. They want to arrange a time for you to come back and talk with them about doing some business. I can't believe all these messages. What were you doing out there today, handing out money?"

Exactly! And, it worked! While I did not discover a secret formula for instant success, I did find a way to attract some new customers. I accomplished this by

35

making friends as opposed to making sales. If you remember what I said earlier about people wanting to do business with other people who are like themselves, now that I had made some friends, I was ready to make some sales. [Please Note-On the reverse side of each voucher, I listed discounts on certain products. The sum of these discounts totaled one hundred dollars.]

INTRODUCING PROJECT FRIENDSHIP

"Project Friendship," or what some describe as the friendship call, is the direct sales approach which I favor. Initially, I recommend that you go out and visit each of the heavy users in your market. Bring with you a "friendship package." This package should consist of an inexpensive gift which your prospect can use. I usually handed out memo pads with my company's name, address and telephone number. Figure Two is an example of this type of gift. The advantage of giving this type of gift is that memo pads are something people can use. And while they are using them, you are getting free advertising because your prospects are staring at the name, address and telephone number of your company.

In Figure Two, the XYZ Company has prominently displayed its name and telephone number—the phone number is represented by the X's in bold type. Notice, at the bottom of the page, there is a subtle advertisement which describes the USP that Tom Tuttle has decided to use in his common sense sales strategy. Tom has also graciously provided his name and telephone number to enable interested prospects to contact him.

In addition to the memo pads, you should provide your prospect with an attractive brochure describing the product(s) you offer. It is important that your brochure include—in addition to a description of your company's products or services—your USP. Remember, in the battle for the hearts and minds of customers, it is important to send a message and reinforce that message. Reinforcement is crucial. While you can alter your choice of advertising media, you must maintain a clear and consistent message. Common sense selling dictates that you need to communicate to your prospects whatever it is that makes you different. <u>Your difference is your edge.</u> And you must take advantage of every opportunity to remind potential customers why you are so special.

Consistency with regard to your choice of message should also be supported by consistency with regard to your transmission of that message. If you select direct sales as part of your overall sales program, then I recommend that you spend at least five hours each week visiting prospects. My suggestion of a minimum of five hours per week is based on the assumption that: 1) you have other important responsibilities which demand your attention and 2) direct selling is not the only component of your sales program. If either of these assumptions are incorrect then you should double the recommended minimum time.

When you make a friendship visit, expect to spend, on average, one to three

FIGURE TWO

MEMO PAD
COMPLIMENTS OF...
THE XYZ COMPANY
3224 Maple Lane
Boise, Idaho 30232
(XXX) XXX-XXXX

DATE:_____

APPOINTMENTS

8:30_____   1:00_____
9:00_____   1:30_____
9:30_____   2:00_____
10:00_____   2:30_____
10:30_____   3:00_____
11:00_____   3:30_____
11:30_____   4:00_____
12:00_____   4:30_____
12:30_____   5:00_____

URGENT   COMPLETED

☐   1._____ ☐
☐   2._____ ☐
☐   3._____ ☐
☐   4._____ ☐
☐   5._____ ☐
☐   6._____ ☐

THE XYZ COMPANY IS THE ONLY COMPANY OFFERING
THE SELF-CALIBRATING WIDGET
AND A ONE YEAR PRODUCT WARRANTY
CONTACT TOM TUTTLE AT XXX-XXXX FOR DETAILS

minutes with each person. Remember, if you do not know this person then your job is to "plant the seed." Do not go with the expectation that your prospect will be waiting, with outstretched arms, to embrace you and your product. Go, instead, with the expectation that this visit will be the first of many you will have with your prospect over the course of what will become a long and mutually profitable business relationship.

If, as you walk through the door, your mind goes blank and you do not know what to say to the person on the other side, allow me to suggest the following:

"Hello. My name is _____ and I am a
representative of_____.
We are a provider of_____.
I wanted to take this opportunity to introduce myself
and present you with this brochure and this gift." [Hand
the person the brochure and the gift] "I believe that our
greatest asset to you would be..........." [Mention your USP]
"After you have had an opportunity to review this brochure,
I would be happy to discuss why I believe our business makes
sense for your business. Thank you for your time, and have a
nice day."

If this is not how you feel comfortable saying it then put it into your own words. The words are unimportant. The purpose of your visit is what counts. And the purpose of your visit is to: 1) introduce yourself, 2) give your prospect your brochure and gift, and 3) mention what makes you so special. This is the objective of your initial contact. [Please Note-Your brochure should summarize the important reasons why your prospect should be doing business with you. It will also reinforce that fact that you were there. In Chapter Eight, I will provide you with an example of this type of a brochure.]

Before you leave, however, you must do one other thing. **Get a business card.** If you see one on a desk or a counter, then take it. If it's displayed then it's meant to be taken. If not, then ask the person you are speaking with for a business card. The business card is extremely important because you will use it to assemble your customer account system. Without a customer account system, you will have no means of recontact other than face-to-face encounters. You need to have other means to contact your prospects. So, whatever you do, get a business card.

THE FOLLOW-UP PROGRAM

I plan to present a program for managing customer satisfaction in Chapter Eleven of this book. The nucleus of this program is customer follow-up. At this point, however, I would like to introduce a different type of follow-up program. This follow-up program is based on the friendship calls you make and the business cards you take. Before entering these business cards into your customer account system (Chapter Ten), you should place them in a "Recontact Holding File." The purpose of this file is to provide you with a list of the customers you have visited. They should be recontacted, by telephone, approximately one week after the date of your initial face-to-face encounter.

The purpose of this recontact is to apply a form of pleasant persistence. You want to reinforce: 1) the fact that you were there, and 2) why you are so special (i.e., your USP). In my case, my Customer Service Manager would make the phone call and it would be as follows:

"Hello. My name is_____and I am the
Customer Service Manager at_____.
Recently, Tony Pattiz, our owner, stopped by. He paid you
a visit to introduce himself and describe _____.
I wanted to take this opportunity to follow-up his visit and
find out if you had any questions?"

The Customer Service Manager took her cue from the prospect. If this person expressed an interest in our product, she arranged an appointment for me to meet with him. If not, she used the follow-up phone call to remind this individual of who we were and why he should consider doing business with us. Since I had determined, prior to my visit, that each prospect is a heavy user and is therefore in need of my product, this follow-up phone call served to reinforce the subtle process of positioning my company as the primary alternative to whoever was currently serving this prospect's needs. As I continued my campaign to attract customers, I was "crowding out" all other potential competitors because I had begun a process of sending a message that was consistent and periodically retransmitted. In Chapter Eight, we will explore how this strategy would work as part of a larger common sense sales campaign.

After the Customer Service Manager hung up, she recorded her impressions of the contact on the back of the business card. These impressions were used to determine each individual's level of interest. A typical comment might be: "Doesn't appear interested now, but could be a prospect sometime in the future." This information was then transferred to this prospect's customer account card (Chapter Ten). The information we had recorded on each prospect's level of interest would be reviewed prior to each recontact.

I SHALL RETURN

At this point, you may be asking the question, "Do I visit the prospect again?" After the telephone follow-up, you determine if there is any interest on the part of your potential customer. Check the back of the business card to see what you or one of your colleagues has written. Then make a list of all the prospects whom you consider to be interested and, like Douglas MacArthur, you vow to return. You should schedule your return visit to be approximately one month after your initial visit. At this point, you come bearing whatever special offer you decide to use. Your choice should be based on your assessment of the market and what you believe would appeal to your customers.

During your return visit, try to have fun. Visualize yourself as Santa Claus handing out presents to a group of needy children. If you're having fun then your enthusiasm will likely become infectious and your prospect will have as much fun receiving your special offer as you have handing it out. Just keeping thinking of Old Saint Nicholas because everybody loves Santa Claus. And, someone who appears as good natured and fun loving as Santa Claus is easy to like. And people who like you may start looking for reasons to have you return. Of course, the reason you want them to discover is to do business with you.

THE SPECIAL TREATMENT

A variation on this theme of Christmas and Santa Claus is what I refer to as "The Special Treatment." Whenever the pressures and hassles of owning and operating my own business became particularly infuriating, I would make a list of my best customers. These were the people whom I enjoyed doing business with and who did a substantial amount of business with me. I would have some memo pads printed with their names, addresses and telephone numbers. I also had the name, address and telephone number of my company conveniently printed at the bottom.

Once I received these pads from the printer, I would jump into my car and visit these people. It was as if I were throwing a surprise party for them. The goodwill--not to mention the business--that resulted from these trips was enormous. The purpose of any special treatment program is to make your best customers feel special. This enables you to build the bonds of genuine friendship. These folks will, as a result of your kindness and consideration, usually stick with you through the good times and the not-so-good times. In other words, <u>don't be afraid to make your customers your friends.</u> I will never forget the words of one friend who told me to call him whenever I was having a slow month. When I asked him why, his response was, "So I can help you out by placing a large order."

Direct selling can be useful to you in your efforts to build your clientele. The important point is: <u>whether you do it as a part of a larger sales campaign or as your principal means of reaching out to new customers, you must do it on a consistent basis</u>. You should visit people whom you consider to be genuinely interested—at regular intervals. Each time you visit them, remind them of who you are and why they should be doing business with you. Maintaining this dialogue will require a certain amount of persistence and effort on your part, but you will quickly establish yourself as someone who cares about other people. And you will become the standard by which these prospects measure all suppliers of your type of product or service. If you combine pleasantness with persistence, they will probably find a reason to do business with you. I seldom had anyone tell me not to come back. And, as long as they left the door open, I knew that there was a sale waiting to happen.

One world of caution: do not neglect your current customers. If "pressing the flesh" appeals to you—and I hope it does—then make time to visit these people as well. Your current customers will be impressed by how much you care about them and their business. While the visit may appear to be a social call, find a way to remind them of what you can do for them and why you are better than the competition. Remember: *pleasant persistence pays off.*

It is now time to introduce the second sales strategy for cultivating new business: **Direct Mail.**

6 A direct mail program that works.

Direct mail is a second common sense sales strategy you can use to interest potential customers in your product. When I mention direct mail, however, people cringe because they think of their own experiences with direct mail. I, like yourself, have had negative experiences with direct mail. I, like yourself, have opened letters or telegrams—only to discover that someone is trying to tell me that I may have won thirty million dollars, but I have definitely won the opportunity to buy some magazines.

In your efforts to attract customers, your goal should be to build a long-term relationship based on trust and likability. There is no place, in this type of a relationship, for dishonesty. You should always assume that your prospect is as honest and intelligent as you. It is unfortunate that the "blue smoke and mirrors" often associated with direct mail has resulted in creating a negative impression in the minds of many regarding any person who identifies himself or herself as a salesperson. You may discover that people sometimes react with hostility toward you because they have had a negative experience with someone who identified himself or herself as a salesperson. Your job is to demonstrate to these people that selling is an honorable profession and that you are an honorable person.

I advocate a direct mail program which is designed to inform instead of deceive. I believe that direct mail, if utilized properly, can serve as a powerful weapon in your sales arsenal. The purpose of your direct mail program should be to build customer awareness and reinforce a message which enables you to stand apart from your competition (i.e., your USP). The purpose of your direct mail program should be to build customer awareness of who you are and what makes you different. To accomplish this, your message must be clear and straightforward. You must believe in yourself and your product. If you do, then do not be afraid to tell others what you have to offer and why it is worth having.

In Figure Three, I provide a sample direct mail piece that our fictitious XYZ Company might use as part of its common sense sales campaign in Boise. This piece is designed to be a three and one-half by five inch postcard. I advocate this size because: 1) it forces you to eliminate any unnecessary words and 2) your prospect is more likely to read something written on a postcard because it is short and to the point.

43

FIGURE THREE

Front Side of the Postcard

XYZ COMPANY
3224 Maple Lane
Boise, Idaho 30232

John Q. Public
3155 Main. Street
Boise, Idaho 30232

Back Side of the Postcard

The XYZ Company introduces its: **self-calibrating widget**

While our company is new to Boise, we have been in the business of manufacturing widgets for over fifty years. With offices in thirty cities and a dozen states, the XYZ Company is committed to manufacturing the finest widgets in the world.

As evidence of our committment, we offer **a standard one-year product warranty on our self-calibrating widget--The longest warranty of any manufacturer in the Boise area.** And now, for a limited time only, we are offering a:

THREE YEAR WARRANTY AT NO ADDITIONAL CHARGE

CALL TOM TUTTLE AT XXX-XXXX FOR DETAILS

Offer expires x/xx/90

Assume that your prospect is like you. I know when I receive a three page letter that begins with, "Mr. Pattiz, I know what a busy man you are and therefore plan to take only a small amount of your time to tell you about a revolutionary new device that is changing lives across America..." I seldom read any farther. This piece of mail is deposited in my circular file to be forwarded to the sanitation department for their reading pleasure!

These three page letters often begin by talking about how important you are and how precious your time is; they then proceed to waste your time with a lot of unnecessary words. You do not want to waste your prospect's time. Actions speak louder than words. If you tell people you do not wish to waste their time, then don't! They will remember your actions—not your words.

When I met managed my business, I met with sales representatives from many other companies. During this period, there was only one occasion when I asked an individual to leave. In this instance, I had told this person I was extremely busy and could only spare ten minutes. I also informed him, that if this were a problem, I would be happy to reschedule our meeting. He indicated it was no problem and then proceeded to spend thirty minutes telling me how he would run my business if he were in charge. He never once mentioned his product. Needless to say, he didn't get the sale. He got the boot!

In Figure Three, XYZ introduces itself and its self-calibrating widget to its target audience. It then proceeds to build credibility by discussing its long history of manufacturing widgets. Building credibility is important and I recommend you determine what strengths you bring to your market. Cite these strengths in your mailer. But remember to keep it simple and straightforward. Your audience is composed of busy decisionmakers who are interested in knowing you are a capable person. These folks do not, however, have the time to read your entire life story. Remember, you are not writing this mailer for your mother to recite at her garden club. Keep it short and to the point.

After initially attempting to build credibility in the minds of its prospects, XYZ introduces its USP. The mailer states:

As evidence of our commitment, **we offer a standard one-year warranty on our self-calibrating widget—The longest warranty of any manufacturer in the Boise area.**

This is important because common sense selling dictates answering the question: "Why should I do business with you?" You should do business with me because <u>I am offering you the longest warranty of any major manufacturer in the Boise area</u>. In the case of one of my mailers, I listed the benefits of doing business with me and then asked my prospect, "Is your current supplier willing to offer you all of these services? If not, then why not?"

Finally, the mailer presents the "Special Offer." I recommend making a special offer if you are relatively new in your marketplace or have not used direct mail before. You want to impress potential customers in the opening round of your battle to win their hearts and minds. You impress them early in order to keep them interested. By offering them a special inducement to try your product, you are creating a special interest and a heightened awareness. In the case of Tom Tuttle and XYZ, Tom wants the prospect to think, the next time he receives a visit, phone call or mailer, "Hey, aren't you the guys offering the three year warranty?"

Some advocate making the special offer or inducement as part of a "loss leader" strategy. This strategy involves selling your product at or below cost for a prescribed period of time. The rationale behind this strategy is that, while you do not make any money, you attract many customers. I do not agree with this approach. Establishing an artificial pricing environment creates an atmosphere of unreality. You know that, if you are to survive, then you will have to raise your prices. Your competitors are making certain your customers know that, if you are to survive, you will have to raise your prices. Once you do raise your prices, the bubble bursts and the competition gleefully tells your customers, "I told you so!" Your credibility goes down the tubes. Besides, why are you in business? If it is to make a profit, then make a profit!

Many larger firms will use a "loss leader" strategy. In their case, however, it may make sense because these firms possess the financial resources to adjust their prices more gradually—thereby reducing the risk of losing their customers. If your job is to sell a product or a service for someone else, you may be thinking that the "loss leader" strategy makes perfect sense for you because you are not the one who will be assuming the loss. Think again. Ask yourself, when the price increase comes as it inevitably will, how prepared you will be to return to these same people and give them the bad news.

I have given you my argument against deceiving a prospect by creating an impression in his mind that he is receiving some item of imaginary value when, in fact, he is being asked to purchase something. This does not mean, however, you cannot use other methods to get his or her attention.

We live in a black and white world. Over ninety percent of what people read is printed on white paper in black ink. If you want to get someone's attention, then simply change the color of your paper or ink—or both. I never had a direct mail piece printed on white paper in black ink. If I used white paper, then I usually selected two ink colors—neither of which were black. If I used black ink, then I selected an exotic type of paper. One time, I even did a mailer using a "hot pink" cardstock.

The important point is that I got the customer's attention. A businessperson seldom leaves a "hot pink" mailer on his or her desk for very long. Colored inks and exotic papers enable your mailer to stand apart from the crowd just as your

USP enables you to stand apart from the crowd. If you decide to use the direct mail approach, then test my hypothesis and be different—at least once.

MAKING YOUR DIRECT MAIL PROGRAM WORK FOR YOU

If your direct mail program is to be effective, then it must be consistent. I recommend a monthly mailer. It is important for this program to be done each month in order to build the necessary awareness among your target group—the heavy users. Take your USP and elaborate on it. A favorite technique of mine is to <u>attach a dollar value to the benefit being offered.</u> In the case of Tom Tuttle and XYZ, Tom could attach a dollar cost to the value of his one-year warranty. He could then show his prospects exactly how much money they would save by purchasing his widgets. This process of attaching a dollar value to your USP enables you to "tangibilize" the intangible by providing your prospect with a concrete dollar value.

Each quarter, a second mailer should offer an incentive or inducement for purchasing your product within a specified time period. Such an offer might involve a discount on selected items or a "buy one get one free" proposal. If you are making a special offer, make certain that you put an expiration date on this offer. You need to do this for two reasons. First, the purpose of this offer is to create an immediate need. Failing to notify your prospects that the offer expires by a certain date encourages them to file it and forget it. Second, without an expiration date, it is conceivable that a customer could walk through the door one year later bearing your offer. Imagine what an embarrassing moment that would be. Make certain an expiration date accompanies all special offers.

In addition to creating an immediate need, the idea of a special offer allows you to "manage the demand" for your product. Your business may be seasonal. You may experience periods when business is slow. During these periods, an incentive program makes sense because it enables you to create a demand for a product which otherwise might not exist. To do this, you should: 1) understand that the demand for a particular product may be cyclical, and 2) increase advertising during these slow periods. Your goal is to minimize the negative effects of a slow season or slack period. A perfect example of this concept would be the efforts of florists to create customer demand through special promotions during periods when people do not typically send each other flowers.

Your choice of a special offer should be based on what you believe will create an immediate need for your product. Know your prospects and what motivates them. Use this information when determining what would be an appropriate incentive to encourage people to purchase your product(s).

When you design your mailer, do not forget to include your USP. What makes you different is your critical marketing advantage and it must appear in everything you say and do.

Designing an effective mail piece is not difficult. Do not reject direct mail simply because you do not consider yourself qualified to design a mailer. There are professionals who can assist you. If you decide to use one of these professionals, then make certain he or she includes your USP and that the mailer does what you want it to do. Do not be afraid, however, to do it yourself.

As an exercise, I challenge you to design a mailer. I have described a "benefits" mailer and a "special offer" mailer. My challenge to you is to design a third type of mail piece for a quarterly mail program. You should consider a mailer which stresses your success and/or competence.

If you decide to adopt a direct mail program, then visit your local post office and find out about a bulk mail permit. This permit will save you a considerable sum of money if you are planning a sizeable mailing.

I have read the findings of several research studies published on the topic of direct mail. Based on this information, the response rate on a typical direct mail program was estimated to be between three and five percent. This means, if you mail to one hundred persons, an estimated three to five people will respond to your mailer. The same studies, however, indicate that if you combine your direct mail program with a telephone follow-up, your response rate will approximately double. It is therefore an appropriate time for me to introduce the third sales strategy for cultivating new business: **Telemarketing.**

A telemarketing program that works.

Telemarketing is a third common sense sales strategy you can use to attract potential customers. Many companies have reported notable success in their use of telephone solicitation programs. A telemarketing program is a program designed to solicit business by telephone. While less personal than a face-to-face encounter, telemarketing is more cost effective. It is also more personal than direct mail because it enables you to answer questions and overcome objections.

When I was younger, I had the opportunity to work for a publishing company. My job was to handle all telephone accounts. These were typically customers and potential customers who were located in geographic areas of the country too costly to visit. Therefore, I contacted these prospects by telephone and attempted to get them to purchase one of our products. As a result of this experience, I learned the importance of telephone selling.

Years later, a friend surprised me with a startling statistic. He worked for an insurance agency and told me that 80% of his agency's business originated from telephone solicitations. His experience reminded me of just how powerful a sales tool the telephone can be.

At this point, you may be saying to yourself, "What happened to making friends instead of making sales. This sounds an awful lot like selling to me." Remember, the litmus test is to ask yourself two very important questions. <u>First, does this sales approach make sense for me? Second, does it feel comfortable?</u> The essence of common sense selling is selling which is sensible and comfortable. It is the application of strategies which enable you to maximize your personal strengths while selling your product(s) or service(s) to others.

Telemarketing has the advantage of being adaptable to your other sales and marketing needs. I will suggest three different types of telemarketing programs. These programs range from making a friend to making an inquiry to making a sale. I recommend that you select the program you believe will work for you.

THE FRIENDLY FOLLOW-UP

The first telemarketing program I recommend is one I introduced in Chapter Five. It involves a follow-up phone call to reinforce a friendly visit. The purpose of this recontact is to apply a form of pleasant persistence. You want to reinforce: 1) the fact that you had spoken and/or met before and 2) why your prospect should be doing business with you (i.e., your USP). This friendly follow-up is a means of letting people know you are interested in them and their business needs. The reason that you give for this recontact, however, is simply to ask if any questions have arisen since your last conversation.

In this type of a telephone contact, I recommend the following script:

"Hello. My Name is _____ and I am the
_____ at _____.
Recently, we spoke regarding _____.
I wanted to take this opportunity to let you know how much
I enjoyed our conversation and to find out if you have any
questions at this time?"

I, or my Customer Service Manager, have used this type of telemarketing script. I do not recall encountering a hostile response from any prospective customers. This approach enables you to demonstrate a friendly concern for your prospects and it is seldom interpreted as an attempt to "twist their arms" in order to make a sale.

There is one variation on this theme which enables you to relate it to a special offer. Let's use Tom Tuttle and XYZ to illustrate:

"Hello. My name is Tom Tuttle and I am the General Manager at
the XYZ Company. Recently, we spoke regarding the one-year
warranty on our self-calibrating widget—the longest warranty
of any supplier in Boise. I wanted to take this opportunity to let
you know how much I enjoyed our conversation and to find out
if you have any questions at this time?"

"You might be interested to know that we are offering a twenty percent
discount on our self-calibrating widgets during March as part of a special
introductory offer. Twenty percent off plus a one-year warranty is a
terrific deal!"

Tom has planted a seed in the mind of his prospect. While not asking for the order, he has made his prospect aware of the special promotion. Thus, in addition to reinforcing Tom's earlier contact and restating his USP, he has created additional interest and hopefully, an immediate need. If Tom really wanted to be bold, he could add the following:

"Why, I decided to put a pencil to this offer and I calculated that an order of one thousand widgets would yield a savings to your company of approximately three hundred dollars!"

Tom has still not asked for the order, but at this point his prospect has either started to get interested or else he has no pulse. Tom is using the friendly follow-up to create a selling opportunity by stimulating his customer's need. This person is a heavy user and therefore has a need for the product. When Tom mentioned the one-year warranty, he sent up a flare. When he discussed the twenty percent discount, he fired off a canon. And when his told his prospect how much he would save by ordering now, he detonated an atomic bomb. Believe me, this person got Tom's message. The ball is now squarely in the prospect's court.

THE INNOCENT INQUIRY

The second telemarketing program I recommend is the innocent inquiry. This program is ideal for someone who is uncomfortable with using the telephone to make a friend or a sale. The purpose of this program is to ask your customer what he or she considers to be important. Let's use Tom Tuttle to demonstrate:

"Hello. My name is Tom Tuttle of the XYZ Company. I realize how busy you are, but I just wanted to take one moment of your time to let you know that my company has introduced the self-calibrating widget into your market along with a one-year warranty—the longest warranty in Boise. The purpose of my call is to find out what else we can do to offer a product which meets all of your needs?"

Have you ever purchased a product, only to later say to yourself, "Just once, I wish they would ask me what's important before they offer one of these things." That's exactly what Tom is doing. He is impressing his prospects with the fact that XYZ considers them so important that they want to consult with them in order to find out how to build a better mouse trap. Or, in our example, a better self-calibrating widget.

This strategy is subtle, but highly effective. Whatever the prospect tells Tom can be used to capture this person's business. If he tells him price is what really matters, then Tom can make a note to call this person back whenever he is offering a discount. If he tells Tom that service or quality are what count, then Tom can emphasize that XYZ stands behind its product with the longest warranty in Boise. Tom has given this individual an opportunity to spell out what he is most concerned about. And, by doing so, if Tom remembers the rules of common sense selling, then his prospect has just created the ideal selling opportunity for Tom!

THE FULL COURT PRESS

Throughout this book, I have assumed that selling is something which may be uncomfortable for you. Therefore, I have suggested strategies designed to take the fear out of selling. I may, however, be doing you an injustice by making this assumption. If this is the case, then my next suggestion may be for you.

The third and final telemarketing program I recommend is the "Full Court Press." This is otherwise known as asking for the appointment. The purpose of this program is to arrange a meeting between you and your prospect. Based on my experience, if you can get the appointment then you have an excellent opportunity to make the sale.

You begin by taking your list of heavy users and contacting them. Your goal is to sell them on you and your product. You may or may not have the opportunity, on the telephone, to get to know these people. The purpose of this contact, however, is to interest them in getting to know you.

Tom Tuttle has graciously volunteered to demonstrate:

"Hello. Is this_____. My name is Tom Tuttle
of XYZ Company. I am calling today to let you know that we are
offering the self-calibrating widget. We believe we can offer you
something you may not currently be getting; namely the longest
product warranty in Boise. We are also offering, for a limited
time only, a twenty percent discount. If quality, reliability
and cost are important to you, then I believe we have much to
offer you. As a matter of fact, I have worked up some projections
on how we can help you to achieve a significant cost savings in
each of these areas. I would very much like to meet with you, at a
time of your convenience, to review these important findings.
When would be a convenient time for us to get together?"

In our example, Tom took a home run swing. He did two things, however, to increase his likelihood of success. First, Tom covered all of the bases—quality, cost and reliability. He gambled that this prospect's "hot button" was somehow linked to one of the major areas which typically concern a customer. Second, Tom stated that he had developed some projections of how he believed he could save this person money in all three areas. Actually, he did no such thing. But it would not be difficult for him to estimate a cost savings based on the product warranty and special discount. The product warranty would address the quality and reliability dimensions cited by Tom while the discount would relate to the cost component.

The prospect could play hardball by indicating to Tom that he was an extremely busy man. He could ask Tom to give him his projections over the phone or mail them to him. Tom, however, would counter this volley by indicating that he would have to meet with this decisionmaker to "fill in some of the blanks" before his projections would be complete. Tom would let his prospect know that if he is interested then he will have to give Tom the appointment. After all, if you are going to the time and trouble of putting together a presentation then you deserve the opportunity to give that presentation and respond to any questions or objections which might arise.

MAJOR ACCOUNT MARKETING

A question arises regarding whether or not it makes sense for you to indicate to each prospect that you have developed some projections you believe he would be interested in seeing. If you use this approach with every prospect, then you will discover that the effort does not always justify the end result. It is unrealistic to devote this much time, energy and effort to each potential customer. You should do so if: 1) the customer has indicated a genuine interest in your product and 2) you would classify him as a heavy user. In this situation, I recommend that you consider a Major Account Marketing Program.

First, you need to determine whether or not an individual or organization qualifies as a "major account." I define a major account as an account whose dollar volume sales would fall in the top twenty percent of all of your accounts dollar volume sales. You must develop your own guidelines, however, regarding what does and does not constitute a "major account."

Second, I contacted potential major accounts and indicated that I understood their business needs and would like to meet with them to demonstrate how I could save them money. Based on my experience, the most persuasive method of getting a potential major account to agree to a meeting is to indicate that you have analyzed their business and believe that you can save them money.

My full court press was on! The terms for discussing how I could save a large account money were that the decisionmaker(s) agree to meet with me. Otherwise, I would be unable to reveal the results of my analysis.

Third, assuming the prospect agreed to a meeting, I would attach a dollar value to my USP. In the case of Tom Tuttle and XYZ, he could attach a dollar value to his one-year warranty. He would then show his prospects exactly how much money would be saved per widget by purchasing his widgets.

This process of attaching a dollar value to your USP enables you to "tangibilize" an intangible item by attaching a concrete dollar value to it. In my case, the intangible benefits I offered were: 1) a guarantee of product quality, 2) free pick-up and delivery, 3) convenient credit terms for approved customers and 4) samples of all customer work kept on file for purposes of easy reordering. I would attempt to estimate a dollar savings based on the size of the potential customer. Let's assume you were using my four selling benefits to interest a major account in your product. Your meeting might go as follows:

> "Mr. Johnson, I mentioned on the telephone that I believed I could save your company money. Let's assume that your organization spends an average of one hundred hours per year delivering the order to the supplier and picking-up the finished product. If we assume an average hourly wage of $4.50, then we could save your company approximately $450.00 per year in this one area alone. Now let's look at product quality and estimate what defective merchandise costs your company each year versus what we can save you by guaranteeing our products against defect...."

What you are doing is simply estimating how much money your USP can save your potential customer. My recommendation is that you make your estimates as realistic as possible. If the dollar savings do not appear to be significant then extend the time period or calculate an inflation factor. Or, bring a calculator with you to your meeting. Let your prospect tell you what he or she estimates the per unit costs on defective merchandise or deliveries and pick-ups to be.

I have two other suggestions regarding what you should bring with you to your meeting with a major account. First, you should provide the account with an attractive brochure describing the product(s) you offer. Enclose a business card—along with your brochure. And make certain the brochure contains your USP.

Second, bring a gift. One possibility would be a set of personalized memo pads. Include your name, address and telephone number on these pads. Also, include your USP. [See Figure Two in Chapter Five for an example.] Remember, in the battle for the hearts and minds of customers, it is important to send a message and reinforce that message. Reinforcement is crucial.

You should use the same techniques to communicate with your largest accounts that you would use to communicate with all users of your product. The difference, however, is that you should spend more time familiarizing yourself with their business needs. A proposal demonstrating how you can save a large account money is an excellent means of accomplishing this task

The battleplan revisited:
Let's put it all together.

Phase One of your battleplan for capturing the hearts and minds of customers requires you to analyze your marketplace in terms of: 1) who the heavy users of your product(s) are and 2) what the strengths and weaknesses of your competition is. Phase Two utilizes this information to create a Unique Selling Proposition (USP). Your USP distinguishes you from the competition by creating a compelling reason as to why people should use your product. Phase Three "puts it all together" in the form of a common sense sales campaign.

It is now time to unveil Phase Three—our comprehensive common sense sales campaign. This campaign combines elements of the direct sales, direct mail and telemarketing programs which we examined in Chapters Five, Six and Seven. Once you have grasped the fundamentals of selling, analyzed your market and decided on the appropriate selling strategies for your business, it is time to "put it all together."

In this chapter, we will return to our familiar example of Tom Tuttle and XYZ. Let's assume that Tom has read *Common Sense Selling*. He understands the "rules of the game" of common sense selling and has asked himself two very important questions. First, does his sales approach make sense? Second, does it feel comfortable?

Tom has chosen a sales campaign based on what he believes will work for him. As we explore his program, you should keep in mind that it is based on one person's application of the strategies and techniques we examined in the previous chapters. Each sales program is different. Therefore, what works for Tom may not necessarily work for you.

REVIEWING THE GROUNDWORK

As stated earlier, Tom Tuttle is now a General Manager for XYZ. His company has just opened an office in Boise, Idaho. Tom has been placed in charge of this office. His product is the self-calibrating widget, which, in reality, is a non-existent device.

In Chapter Two, we discussed the factors of success and the importance of an action plan. Let's assume Tom knows what factors of success influence his business. He has formulated an appropriate action plan to achieve these success goals. Remember, however, that Tom's primary responsibility will be sales-related. Therefore, his goal is to build a market in Boise for his company's product.

Tom's company has provided him with information on the heavy users in his marketplace. Nonetheless, he does have one major problem. His company has no name recognition in Boise. Therefore, his job is similar to the job of someone who is starting a brand new business.

If Tom has no name recognition then one of the objectives of his common sense sales campaign will be to build credibility. He needs to assure potential customers that his company is capable of manufacturing self-calibrating widgets which will meet their needs. This is important because his competition may combat any inroads he attempts to make in Boise by discrediting him. They can do this by emphasizing their experience and record of reliability while casting doubts on XYZ's ability to do the job. It is Tom's responsibility to allay any fears potential customers may have regarding his company's ability and experience. He must convince his prospects that he can do the job. This can be done as part of his common sense sales campaign.

The XYZ Company has offices in thirty cities and a dozen states. Tom has learned that XYZ is larger than any of its competitors in Boise. Therefore, he can emphasize the size of his organization to ease any fears potential customers might have regarding XYZ's ability and experience. [Please Note-In your case, you may not be the largest. As a matter of fact, if you are starting out on your own then you may be the smallest. Nevertheless, you are the sum total of your experience. Anticipate any doubts potential customers may have regarding your ability to do the job. Use previous experience or training to reassure these customers. Remember, one of the goals of your common sense sales campaign will be to remove your prospects doubts about you.]

Now that Tom has addressed this issue of credibility, he can develop his USP. He knows his objective is to distinguish himself from his major competitors by offering customers something his competition is not offering them. To do this, Tom asks himself three very important questions: <u>1) Is there something I am offering that the majority of my competitors are not offering, 2) Is there a perceived weakness on the part of my competition which I can exploit or 3) Can I array my strengths in such a manner as to differentiate myself from my competition?</u>

Tom has answered these questions by conducting a "competitor analysis" (Chapter Four). As a result of this analysis, he has discovered three interesting facts. First, the price of XYZ's self-calibrating widget is comparable with that of their major competitors in Boise. Second, there is no significant difference in quality or price. Third, all of the companies Tom spoke with stated that there is no formal warranty beyond the ninety-day warranty for parts and labor.

It is with regard to this third variable, which I shall label service reliability, that Tom senses an opportunity. The other major suppliers of self-calibrating widgets have determined that the costs of providing a one-year warranty are greater than the benefits. Tom's company, however, has always offered a standard one-year warranty and an optional three-year warranty. For XYZ, the benefits associated with this warranty have traditionally outweighed the costs. If Tom can use his sales and marketing program to emphasize the fact that XYZ offers a longer warranty on its product than any other supplier in the Boise market, then he can separate himself from his competitors.

Tom has decided that his USP is the one-year warranty offered by XYZ. He therefore needs to create a reason why this one-year warranty is worth having (i.e., "tangibilize" an intangible benefit). He has decided to attach a dollar value to his benefit. Tom believes, that by attaching a dollar value to the one-year warranty, his prospects will consider it to be something worth having.

To attach a dollar value to this product, Tom has done some research on the life expectancy of the average self-calibrating widget. He has gathered research findings which indicate that a one-year warranty extends the life of the product by an additional year. This finding is based on published studies of widgets regularly serviced during their first year of operation.

THE SALES CAMPAIGN

Tom is now ready to unveil his sales campaign. This campaign will utilize direct sales, direct mail and telemarketing. These three selling mediums will reinforce each other and, more importantly, the message Tom plans to send to his target audience. His message is:

THE XYZ COMPANY IS NOW BOISE'S LARGEST MANUFACTURER OF SELF-CALIBRATING WIDGETS. OUR SIZE IS A DIRECT RESULT OF OUR EXPERIENCE IN BUILDING A SUPERIOR PRODUCT. SINCE WE ARE THE LARGEST AND SINCE WE BUILD THE BEST PRODUCT, WE CAN AFFORD TO OFFER THE LONGEST PRODUCT WARRANTY OF ANY SUPPLIER IN BOISE. A LONGER PRODUCT WARRANTY MEANS A LONGER PRODUCT LIFE SPAN AND THEREFORE LOWER PRODUCT COSTS.

Tom Tuttle has targeted five hundred potential customers. These customers are businesses that use his product in sufficient quantities and with sufficient regularity to enable XYZ to achieve its desired objectives in Boise. [Please Note-I will discuss setting objectives and monitoring performance in the next chapter.]

The five hundred businesses Tom has targeted will form the focal point of XYZ's common sense sales campaign. Tom has devised a plan to capture these businesses. By sending a message and reinforcing this message to this audience,

Tom believes he will succeed in: 1) capturing a sufficient share of this market to achieve XYZ's desired objectives and 2) positioning his company as either the primary supplier or self-calibrating widgets or the primary alternative to whoever is currently supplying these businesses with self-calibrating widgets.

Month One: The Introduction And The Special Offer

During Month One, Tom's goal will be to introduce himself and his company to potential customers. To accomplish this task, he has planned to visit each of these businesses. He plans to spend three and one-half days each week making "friendship" calls. Tom's objective is to visit each of his five hundred prospects during Month One. Each week, he will start visiting prospects on Monday afternoon and complete his visits on Thursday afternoon. Tom believes that his prospects will need Monday mornings to organize their tasks for the week ahead and Fridays to plan their weekends. Therefore, a face-to-face encounter on Monday mornings or Fridays would yield less than optimal results because Tom would not have his prospects undivided attention.

Tom has decided that, during Month One, he will offer potential customers the opportunity to have a three-year standard warranty—as opposed to the one-year standard warranty he would normally offer them. This three-year offer, however, will only be on orders of one hundred or more widgets because Tom wants to provide his prospects with an incentive for placing a large order.

The offer will be communicated to each prospect verbally. It will also be contained in an attractive two-color, bi-fold brochure which Tom plans to give each prospect. This brochure—minus its attractive colors and stylish paper—is represented by Figure Four.

Tom also plans to present each prospect with three complimentary memo pads (Figure Five). These memo pads will serve to reinforce the message XYZ wants to send to all of its potential customers. These pads will provide Tom with free advertising because they are an item his prospects are likely to use. And, while they are using the pads, they will be reminded of why they should be doing business with Tom Tuttle and his company.

In Figures Four and Five, Tom has taken the message he planned to send to his target audience:

THE XYZ COMPANY IS NOW BOISE'S LARGEST MANUFACTURER OF SELF-CALIBRATING WIDGETS. OUR SIZE IS A DIRECT RESULT OF OUR EXPERIENCE IN BUILDING A SUPERIOR PRODUCT. SINCE WE ARE THE LARGEST AND SINCE WE BUILD THE BEST PRODUCT, WE CAN AFFORD TO OFFER THE LONGEST PRODUCT WARRANTY OF ANY SUPPLIER IN BOISE. A LONGER PRODUCT WARRANTY MEANS A LONGER PRODUCT LIFE SPAN AND THEREFORE LOWER PRODUCT COSTS.

FIGURE FOUR : THE OUTSIDE OF THE XYZ COMPANY'S SALES BROCHURE

(BACK COVER OF THE BROCHURE)   (FRONT COVER OF THE BROCHURE)

MAPLE LANE

XYZ COMPANY

ELM ST.

OUR OFFICE IS LOCATED AT:

3224 Maple Lane
Boise, Idaho 30232
(XXX) XXX-XXXX

THE XYZ COMPANY

WE'RE THE LARGEST SUPPLIER OF
SELF-CALIBRATING WIDGETS
IN BOISE
AND WE'VE GOT
THE WARRANTY TO PROVE IT!

THE LONGEST
STANDARD WARRANTY
OF ANY SUPPLIER IN BOISE

WE'RE THE PEOPLE TO CALL
AND OUR NUMBER IS:
(XXX) XXX-XXXX

WHO IS XYZ COMPANY?

We are one of the leading manufacturers of self calibrating widgets in the United States.

WHAT WE CAN OFFER YOU:

- Thirty offices in twelve states

- Fifty years of manufacturing experience

- A team of product experts who make it their business to know your business

WHO WE CAN OFFER YOU:

- Tom Tuttle, General Manager, with eleven years of full-time, professional experience enabling him to work with you to ensure that our product meets your needs

- A professional staff of over one-hundred people who specialize in marketing, planning, manufacturing, and customer service

WHY WE MAKE SENSE FOR YOU:

- Because we are dedicated to building a better product that will save your business money.

- As proof of our dedication and our success, we offer you the longest product warranty of any major supplier in Boise, Idaho

---

A WARRANTY
BY ANY OTHER NAME
IS JUST A WARRANTY

OR IS IT?

Last year, several industry sources estimated that the average user of self-calibrating widgets spent **TWELVE HUNDRED DOLLARS** to replace worn out or defective units. These are units that would not have had to be replaced last year if they had only lasted <u>one additional year</u>.

At XYZ Company, we believe we build the finest self-calibrating widget on the market. And we back our belief with the **<u>longest product warranty of any supplier in Boise</u>**

When you buy one of our self-calibrating widgets, we provide you with a standard **one-year warranty.** A warranty which several experts agree will extend the life of your self-calibrating widgets by <u>at least one additional year.</u> Based on articles published in Widget World and other authoritative sources, our widgets are capable of lasting at least <u>one additional year</u> at an estimated savings to your company of **TWELVE HUNDRED DOLLARS** per one thousand widgets.

And, for a limited time only, on orders of 100 or more, we are extending our standard warranty to a **FULL THREE YEARS**. Simply call **xxx-xxxx** or bring in this coupon and receive an additional two years of guaranteed coverage at no additional charge. Your savings has just tripled to **THIRTY-SIX HUNDRED DOLLARS** per 1,000 widgets

THIS OFFER EXPIRES XX/XX/90

And he has translated this message into a powerful, yet simple selling slogan that will enable him to make the following points: 1) XYZ is the largest supplier in the Boise market and therefore possesses the ability and experience to serve the needs of this market and 2) XYZ offers a superior warranty and therefore possesses a superior product. All of this is implied in Tom's USP:

WE'RE THE LARGEST SUPPLIER OF
SELF-CALIBRATING WIDGETS
AND WE'VE GOT
THE WARRANTY TO PROVE IT!

Inside the brochure, Tom explains what this warranty means to potential customers by attaching a concrete dollar value to it. Tom states:

> Last year, several industry sources estimated that the average user of self-calibrating widgets spent **TWELVE HUNDRED DOLLARS** to replace worn out or defective units. These are units which would not have had to be replaced last year if they had only lasted <u>one additional year</u>.

> When you buy one of our self-calibrating widgets, we provide you with a standard one-year warranty. A warranty that several experts agree will extend the life of your self-calibrating widgets by one additional year. Based on articles published in Widget World and other authoritative publications, our widgets are capable of lasting at least <u>one additional year</u> at an estimated savings to your company of **TWELVE HUNDRED DOLLARS** per one thousand widgets.

Tom then explains why he believes his organization can meet the needs of its customers. He does this in clear and concise language when he answers the questions: 1) What we can offer you, 2) Who we can offer you and 3) Why we make sense for you. It is important for Tom to communicate his information in a clear and concise manner. People are not interested in long-winded statements which ramble on about a company's history or what it can offer its customers. Keep it short and to the point.

When Tom enters a prospect's business, his goal is to: 1) introduce himself, 2) hand his prospect the gift and 3) state his USP—XYZ is the largest supplier of self-calibrating widgets and has the warranty to prove it! He must also remember to pick-up a business card before he leaves.

Tom's three-minute greeting would be as follows:

FIGURE FIVE

MEMO PAD
COMPLIMENTS OF...
THE XYZ COMPANY
3224 Maple Lane
Boise, Idaho 30232
(XXX) XXX-XXXX

DATE:_____

APPOINTMENTS

8:30_____   1:00_____
9:00_____   1:30_____
9:30_____   2:00_____
10:00_____   2:30_____
10:30_____   3:00_____
11:00_____   3:30_____
11:30_____   4:00_____
12:00_____   4:30_____
12:30_____   5:00_____

URGENT   COMPLETED

☐ 1._____ ☐
☐ 2._____ ☐
☐ 3._____ ☐
☐ 4._____ ☐
☐ 5._____ ☐
☐ 6._____ ☐

WE'RE THE LARGEST SUPPLIER OF
SELF-CALIBRATING WIDGETS
IN BOISE
AND WE'VE GOT
THE WARRANTY TO PROVE IT!
CALL: (XXX) XXX-XXXX FOR DETAILS

"Hello. My name is Tom Tuttle and I am the General Manager of The XYZ Company. I wanted to stop by today and introduce myself. I also wanted to give you this brochure and gift."
[He hands his prospect the brochure and gift.] "We are now the largest supplier of self-calibrating widgets in Boise and offer the longest product warranty of any supplier in town. After you have had an opportunity to read this brochure, I hope you will give me the opportunity to meet with you again because I believe that my product makes sense for your business. Before I leave, I would like to pick-up a business card."

"Thank-you for your time and have a nice day."

If the prospect, or more likely, the dreaded gatekeeper asks Tom why he wants a business card then he simply replies, "From time to time we offer special discounts on our product and I don't want you to miss any opportunity to save money by taking advantage of one of these discounts."

As soon as Tom departs, he will record his impressions of this face-to-face encounter on the back of the business card. When he returns to his office, Tom places these cards in a recontact holding file. If you remember, he is not making any visits on Monday mornings or Fridays. On Monday mornings, he is organizing his weekly schedule. On Fridays, he is making his friendly follow-up telephone calls.

As indicated in Chapter Seven, the purpose of the friendly follow-up is to apply a form of pleasant persistence. Each Friday, Tom is calling the people whom he visited during the previous week. He wants to reinforce: 1) the fact that he made the visit and 2) why XYZ is so special. In Tom's case, his telemarketing script for this friendly follow-up is:

"Hello. Is this_____? My name is Tom Tuttle and I am the General Manager of XYZ Company. I stopped by earlier in the week to introduce myself and my company. I was calling today to find out if you had a chance to read the brochure I dropped off and if you had any questions about it?"

[Tom always takes his cue from his prospect. Let's assume that this person indicates he has not read the brochure.]

"Well, I know how busy you must be, but I also know how important product costs are to you. I believe that my product makes sense for your company and I am convinced that I can save you money because my company is the largest supplier of self-calibrating widgets and offers the longest warranty on those widgets of any supplier in this market. I would therefore very much like to have your business."

"Thank-you for your time and have a nice day."

Tom has told his prospect why he should be doing business with XYZ (i.e., his USP). He has also tried to convey a sense of enthusiasm in his voice because he wants the prospect to be asking himself the question, "Why isn't my current supplier working this hard for me?" Or, "Why doesn't my current supplier offer me this one-year warranty?"

Remember, if Tom is to use the common sense selling rules which I outlined in Chapter Three then he must be given the opportunity to make a sale. In order to create this opportunity, he needs to have his prospect say to himself, "This guy may have something that is of value to me." Or, "This guy may have the answer to my problem." If Tom can create a high level of interest then he can build a bridge between what he has to offer and what his prospects need to have.

<u>Month Two: The Direct Mail Campaign And The Second Telephone Contact, But The Song Remains The Same.</u>

Once Tom has introduced himself, his company and his product to the target audience, he needs to begin the process of reinforcement. Beginning with Month Two, he will re-transmit the same message to his target audience. He will change his style of transmission—alternating between our three primary sales mediums. But the song remains the same.

At the beginning of Month Two, Tom will send his first direct mail piece to the target audience. This mailer will be almost identical to the brochure he distributed during Month One. Remember, Tom has been recontacting each of his prospects as part of the friendly follow-up program. The purpose of this follow-up was to reinforce: 1) the fact that he made the visit and 2) why XYZ is so special.

The purpose of the follow-up is to rekindle each prospect's memories of his earlier encounter with Tom. Between Tom's face-to-face encounter and his telephone recontact, however, the prospects may have discarded the brochure they were given. Since Tom's goal is to get each prospect to take a second look at him and his prospect, it makes sense to send them a second brochure. The only changes Tom has made to the brochure were made to prepare it for the mail and to extend the initial special offer by an additional forty-five days.

During the first half of Month Two, Tom will wait for his target audience to receive this mailer. While he is waiting, he will be building his customer account system. Each prospect is recorded on a special card. This card is cross-filed by business name and industry type. Henceforth, each time Tom contacts a prospect, he will be able to record his impressions of that contact on the card. In Chapter Ten, I will unveil a sample "Customer Account Card" and outline a program for building a customer account system.

During the second half of Month Two, Tom will speak with each of his prospects by telephone. The purpose of his second telemarketing program will be to inquire if his target audience received the mailer. The first telemarketing program was a friendly follow-up. This one will be an innocent inquiry. Tom's real objective, however, is to reinforce his message and increase customer awareness of the strengths of XYZ's product versus that of its competition.

The telemarketing script for his innocent inquiry is as follows:

"Hello. May I speak with_____. Hello. This is
Tom Tuttle with XYZ. I was calling today to find out is you
received our mailer with the special offer extending our product
warranty—already the longest of any supplier in Boise—by an
additional two years?"

[Let's assume that the prospect indicates he has received it,
but does not know if he is interested at this time.]

"Well, that's understandable. You are a prudent businessperson
and need to evaluate each proposal carefully. I just wanted to
call you today to let you know what a tremendous savings you
can realize on this offer. As a matter of fact, I estimate that a
three-year warranty would save your company THIRTY-SIX
HUNDRED DOLLARS per one thousand widgets. We weren't
kidding when we said we're the largest supplier of self-
calibrating widgets and we've got the warranty to prove it!
But, I've taken up enough of your time. It was good to talk to
you again. I hope to be hearing from you soon because I'd like
to be your supplier of self-calibrating widgets. Thank-you once
again for your time."

In this script, Tom launches into his sales pitch when he tells a seemingly disinterested prospect what a fantastic deal XYZ is offering him. Then Tom retreats, almost as if to say, "I want your business, but this is such a good offer that I have other people waiting to place their orders." He concludes by telling his prospect that he would like to be his supplier of self-calibrating widgets.

In this telephone encounter, Tom has decided that he is going to have the last word. This is important because he does not want an unenthusiastic prospect to misinterpret his periodic contacts as a sign of desperation. Tom knows he needs to exude a sense of confidence in order to create the impression of a winner. His response to his prospect's disinterest is to express his own disbelief.

Month Three: A Second Face-To-Face Encounter, A Second Mailer And A Thank-You To The True Believers.

During Month Three, Tom's primary objective is to begin "crowding out" his competition. What makes him different is not the fact that he is persistent. Nor is it the fact that he is consistent. What makes Tom different is the fact that he is <u>both</u> persistent and consistent. He is periodically recontacting each prospect with the same basic message. By adopting this strategy, he will reduce the possibility of getting lost in the clutter. Remember, each of Tom's prospects is being bombarded daily with messages about numerous products and services. Despite this fact, some companies succeed. Their success is attributable to their ability to break through the clutter. Their message does not get lost. By sending the same message on a periodic basis, Tom is increasing the likelihood that his message will not get lost.

It is important, however, to distinguish between the message and the messenger. You hold your prospect's interest by changing the messenger. This is accomplished by varying your sales mediums or altering the format of a particular medium. An example of this technique is direct mail. If you were to send the same message in the same manner each month then your audience would develop a recognition of your message. Once they saw that familiar green postcard with purple ink they would realize who the sender was. And, since they had identified the messenger, they would also assume they knew his message and likely discard your mailer without reading it.

On the other hand, if each mail piece were in a different color ink and on a different type of paper, then your audience would not know what you were planning to tell them because they would not know that it was your message. To find out who sent the message, they would have to read it.

Remember, you change the type of messenger and the special inducement (e.g., twenty-percent off, buy one get one free) in order to keep your prospect interested in you and what you have to offer. You send the same USP, however, so your prospect is able to distinguish you from all the other people who are competing for his attention. You succeed in being different while, in fact, remaining the same. And, by doing so, you create an interested prospect and send an uncluttered message.

During Month Three, Tom plans to "crowd out" his competitors by returning to the "scene of the crime." This is otherwise known as revisiting his prospects. Tom will not, however, be revisiting all of these people.

Month Three is the beginning of what I shall refer to as "selective discrimination." This process is based on the level of interest each prospect has demonstrated thus far. Remember, Tom assumes his target audience is composed of heavy users capable of purchasing his product in sufficient quantity and with sufficient regularity to enable XYZ to achieve its sales and profit objectives. Nonetheless, he needs to to narrow the field based on how interested each prospect appears to be. His objective, by the end of Year One, is: 1) To capture a sufficient share of this market to achieve XYZ's desired objectives and 2) To position his company as either the primary supplier of self-calibrating widgets or the primary alternative to whoever is supplying self-calibrating widgets to each of his prospects. The process of selective discrimination enables him to determine whether he can capture a given customer or become the primary substitute to his current supplier.

Tom's most precious resource is his time. By selectively discriminating, he focuses his time on prospects who have demonstrated some interest in him and his product. These people represent the target group within the target group because they are the folks whom Tom has determined are winnable if he devotes the necessary time, energy and effort.

During Month Three, Tom will revisit the people he considers to be winnable. Tom will enter each place of business and use the following approach:

"Hello. It's good to see you again. I just wanted to stop by today to make certain the literature that we sent you has answered all of your questions regarding how our warranty can save your business money and why our product makes sense for you."

"You know, when I stopped by the last time, I was so impressed with your organization that I'm afraid I forgot to give you one of my cards." [Tom intentionally did not hand out business cards on his earlier visit. He did not need to because his name, address and telephone number were contained in the brochure. His failure, to hand out business cards, however, provides him with a convenient reason to return.]

"We've had a positive response in this area as a result of offering the longest warranty of any supplier in Boise. As a matter of fact, tripling our standard warranty coverage as part of our special introductory offer was probably something XYZ regrets doing because of the strong response to our one-year warranty. But I'm glad I was able to convince them to do it because it means a greater savings to you."

[Let's assume the prospect is not buying today.]

"Well, I just wanted to stop by once again to make certain you didn't feel that you were being ignored. You know, I'd like to have you join our family of satisfied customers and the reason that I came back is to let you know that we care. It's good to see you again. Thank-you for your time and have a nice day."

Tom has let his prospect know that he considers his business to be very important. He has reminded this person why he should be doing business with XYZ. He has also attempted to create an impression in the mind of his prospect that he is on the side of the customer. He builds this trust by cleverly stating:

"As a matter of fact, tripling our standard warranty coverage as part of our special introductory offer was probably something XYZ regrets doing because of the strong response to our one-year warranty. But I'm glad I was able to convince them to do it   because it means a greater savings to you."

Now the prospect believes that he and Tom are working together to get the best possible deal from XYZ. Tom is using the "I'm on your side" approach to build the confidence of his potential customers. This is a theme he can continue to use in future contacts with customers.

As you might surmise, I cannot provide you with every possible response to every conceivable objection a prospect may pose. I do advise, however, that you take your cue from the other person. Tom's strategy is based on his experience in classifying customer responses into specific categories. This strategy assumes that each type of customer response should elicit an appropriate counter-response. For example, if this person responds with disinterest then Tom counters with his own disbelief. If the prospect responds with interest then Tom counters with enthusiasm. And so on. You should determine what signal your prospect is sending you and respond accordingly. With experience, you will be surprised at just how easy this task will become.

At the end of Month Three, Tom will be sending out two mailers. The first will be part of his monthly direct mail program. This mailer will be sent to all five hundred businesses. This mailer will thank these businesses for their enthusiastic response to the special introductory offer. Tom wants to create, in the mind of each prospect, the perception that this offer was so successful that XYZ felt obliged to thank its customers. Tom wants these people to be saying to themselves, once they have read this mailer, "This offer must have been better than I originally thought if they're going to the trouble and expense of thanking people. Maybe I need to take a second look at it." Figure Six represents this mailer.

The second mailer will be sent to a more select audience. It will be sent to all the people who have done business with XYZ during the first three months. This mailer is also a thank-you. This mailer, however, is intended to let these people know that their business is greatly appreciated. A thank-you is a simple, yet powerful gesture. It can help you build the bonds of genuine friendship. Expressing thanks to your customers may prove to be your most effective common sense sales technique. Figure Seven represents this mailer.

In the final analysis, while your USP is a method for initially distinguishing yourself from the competition, what will really enable you to stand apart is your ability to demonstrate that you care about your customers and that you are capable of providing them with good service. In Chapter Eleven, I will introduce a program intended to accomplish this objective.

Month Four: Moving From An Interest To An Appointment.

Tom has spent his first three months building an awareness of himself and his product. The purpose of his direct sales, direct mail and telemarketing efforts have been to create an awareness of and interest in his product. Tom has attempted to create a "selling opportunity." In Month Four, he will ask for the order.

Asking for the order is not an "all or nothing" proposition. What I mean is if you ask for the sale and the prospect says no, do not automatically destroy his file, remove him from your contact programs and avoid him on the street. Unless a prospect indicates that he never wants you to contact him again, do not assume he has rejected you or your product.

Your approach should be based on whether the prospect demonstrates his interest is low, moderate or high. If it is low, then your goal should be to periodically remind him that you are ready to serve his needs should his current supplier fail him. A periodic reminder might involve a monthly mailer plus a telephone call once every three months. If his interest is moderate, then your goal should be to increase his level of interest by demonstrating that your product meets his needs and that you care about his business. This might involve a monthly mailer and a monthly phone call or visit. If his interest is high, then you should ask for the order. This means asking for an appointment to discuss a long-term business relationship. Remember, your decision should be based on how interested your prospect appears to be. Trust your instincts because there are no scientific formulas to gauge an individual's level of interest. And, there is no penalty for a wrong guess.

In Month Four, Tom will contact those individuals whom he has rated as

FIGURE SIX

Front of the XYZ Mailer

XYZ COMPANY
3224 Maple Lane
Boise, Idaho 30232

John Q. Public
3155 Main. Street
Boise, Idaho 30232

Back of the XYZ Mailer

THE XYZ COMPANY THANKS YOU

WE'RE THE LARGEST SUPPLIER
OF SELF-CALIBRATING WIDGETS
IN BOISE AND WE'VE GOT
THE WARRANTY TO PROVE IT!

We have been overwhelmed by your decision
to try our limited offer of a three-year warranty.
We realize that you had a choice
and we thank-you for choosing us.

If we can be of further assistance, do not hesitate to
call us at: (XXX) XXX-XXXX

FIGURE SEVEN

XYZ'S THANK-YOU NOTE TO THEIR BEST CUSTOMERS

AT THE XYZ COMPANY,
WE WOULD LIKE TO TAKE THIS OPPORTUNITY
TO THANK-YOU
FOR PURCHASING OUR
SELF-CALIBRATING WIDGET.

WE REALIZE THAT YOU HAD A CHOICE
AND WE ARE GRATEFUL THAT YOU CHOSE US.

WE'RE THE LARGEST SUPPLIER
OF SELF-CALIBRATING WIDGETS
IN BOISE AND WE'VE GOT
THE WARRANTY TO PROVE IT!

XYZ COMPANY IS LOCATED AT
3224 MAPLE LANE
BOISE, IDAHO 30232
(XXX) XXX-XXXX

having a high level of interest in XYZ and its self-calibrating widgets. Tom will use a form of the "full court press" by indicating he is convinced he can save his prospect money and would like to meet with this individual to discuss a long-term business relationship.

Tom has decided to offer these prospects a cash savings program based on high volume purchases. Since his target audience is composed of heavy users, a cash savings program based on large volume purchases is a sensible approach. It is also an ideal method for "locking in" a long-term relationship with a heavy user. [While your business may not be able to offer such a program, you should consider any program which enables you to "lock in" large customers based on a perceived value or benefit that you are capable of providing them.]

Tom's telemarketing script for his "full court press" is as follows:

"Hello. May I speak with_____. Hello.
This is Tom Tuttle with XYZ. How are you today?"

"I wanted to touch base with you today because I have been
studying your company's needs. I would like to propose a
Volume Purchasing Program. This program would enable
you to realize a significant cash savings on large volume
purchases. And, this savings would be in addition to the
savings you would already receive on our one-year warranty—
the longest of any supplier in Boise. Based on our previous
discussions, I got the impression that our warranty was an
item which you considered to be a plus. I now believe that
a Volume Purchasing Program would give us a solid basis for
sitting down and determining if XYZ is the logical choice to
be your supplier of self-calibrating widgets. When would be
a convenient time for us to get together?"

Tom has told his prospect that he considers him to be interested in XYZ's widget. If his assessment is correct, then he has given this person an additional reason to transform his interest into a business relationship. If Tom gets the appointment, he will use it to learn more about his prospect. Tom will attempt to find a common area of interest with his prospect. He will use this opportunity to build a bridge between what he has to offer and what his prospect needs to have.

What if his Tom's prospect indicates that he is not interested in a meeting. Tom would respond as follows:

"Well, I am sorry that we will not have the opportunity to meet
at this time. I believe such a meeting would have enabled me to
learn more about you and discover additional ways in which XYZ

could save your business money."

"Nevertheless, I realize what a busy person you are and I hope we will have the opportunity to meet at some future date. If I can be of any assistance, please do not hesitate to contact me. We offer a technical assistance program for everyone—whether they are currently doing business with us or not."

Tom has left the door open for a future meeting. He has also indicated to his prospect that he would still be happy to assist him in answering any questions or solving any problems which might arise. You may think Tom is foolish to offer assistance to someone who is currently unwilling to do business with him. This is not so. If his prospect were to call with a question or a problem, he would be giving Tom an additional opportunity to capture his business by demonstrating that he cares about this person. By portraying himself as a concerned problem solver, even if Tom fails to make the sale, he succeeds in creating goodwill. And goodwill, like faith, can move mountains when it comes to converting an interest into a sale.

During Month Four, Tom also plans to send out his third monthly mailer. Remember, in Month Two he launched his direct mail program. This program established the minimal contact requirements between Tom and his prospects. In Month Two, the mailer was a reprint of Tom's brochure and it contained a special offer. In Month Three, it was a thank you intended to create a perception of success as a result of an unbeatable offer. In Month Four, Tom plans to send out a mailer emphasizing competence.

He has contacted three people who have done business with XYZ. These people indicated during the regular customer follow-up (Chapter Eleven) that they were pleased with the product and with the concern XYZ had demonstrated for their business needs. Tom, therefore, recontacted them to request their permission to reprint these favorable comments in a monthly mailer. He indicated that they would be receiving free publicity as well. Not surprisingly, all three gladly consented.

The mailer is illustrated by Figure Eight. It represents a two-color, bifold. This mailer contains some of the same information which was used in the original brochure. Nonetheless, Tom has changed his ink colors, paper type and revised a part of the contents. Remember, his goal is to be different while remaining the same. And, by doing so, create an interested prospect and send an uncluttered message.

Month Five: "Getting To Know You, Getting To Know All About You."

By Month Five, we should assume Tom's aggressive common sense sales campaign has begun to pay-off. As a result of his persistence and consistence, he

THE XYZ COMPANY

WE'RE THE LARGEST SUPPLIER OF
SELF-CALIBRATING WIDGETS
IN BOISE
AND WE'VE GOT
THE WARRANTY TO PROVE IT!

THE LONGEST
STANDARD WARRANTY
OF ANY SUPPLIER IN BOISE

Maple Lane

XYZ Company

Elm St.

OUR OFFICE IS LOCATED AT:
3224 Maple Lane
Boise, Idaho 30232
(XXX) XXX-XXXX

WE'RE THE PEOPLE TO CALL
AND OUR NUMBER IS:

(XXX) XXX-XXXX

WHO IS XYZ COMPANY?

We are one of the leading manufacturers of self calibrating widgets in the United States.

WHAT WE CAN OFFER YOU:

- Thirty offices in twelve states

- Fifty years of manufacturing experience

- A team of product experts who make it their business to know your business

WHO WE CAN OFFER YOU:

- Tom Tuttle, General Manager, with eleven years of full-time, professional experience that enables him to work with you to ensure that our product meets your needs

- A professional staff of over one-hundred people who specialize in marketing, planning, manufacturing, and customer service

WHY WE MAKE SENSE FOR YOU:

- Because we are dedicated to building a better product that will save your business money.

- As proof of our dedication and our success, we offer you the longest product warranty of any major supplier in Boise, Idaho

WHAT SOME OF OUR CUSTOMERS ARE SAYING ABOUT US

Ralph Torgensen of HIJ Company had this to say:

"When Tom Tuttle told me about his product, I thought it was simply too good to be true. Boy was I wrong!"

Pete Stewart of LMN Company had this to say:

"The attention and concern that XYZ has shown for me and my business has been just terrific! I couldn't be any happier."

Glen Brewster of OPQ Company had this to say:

"The money that my company has saved on product costs in just three months is enough to pay my salary for a full year."

WE INVITE YOU TO JOIN OUR FAMILY OF SATISFIED CUSTOMERS

FIND OUT WHY OUR BUSINESS MAKES SENSE FOR YOUR BUSINESS

CALL TOM TUTTLE AT XXX-XXXX FOR DETAILS

is attracting new customers. And these customers are people whom he would like to get to know better. Therefore, Tom has hired an employee. Her name is Tina.

Initially, Tom was able to operate his office by himself. While he was away, his message machine recorded all telephone calls and inquiries. Now, however, his clientele is growing and he must therefore spend more of his time with his current customers; making certain their business needs are being met.

He must visit these people for a second reason as well. "Pressing the flesh" is an excellent means of getting an additional orders. If Tom periodically visits his best customers, they will think self-calibrating widgets each time they see him. If these customers need to place an order, but are too busy, Tom's presence will give them a reason and an opportunity to do so. Tom wants these people--who pay the bills--to affectionately think of him as Mr. Widget.

If you are like Tom, you may discover that, as your customer base grows, it will become increasingly important to spend more time with your larger accounts. You may therefore decide to hire someone who can answer telephone inquiries and handle walk-in traffic. You should select someone who possesses good interpersonal skills because you may decide to delegate your direct mail and telemarketing responsibilities to this individual. As my business grew, my Customer Service Manager was trained to do telemarketing and direct mail. I spent much of my time visiting current and prospective customers.

Tom's goal is to get to know his important customers. By getting to know these people, he becomes a part of their extended business family. He is the man who cares about them. He is the man who is building a relationship based on trust and likability. He is the man who is always looking for ways to assist them.

During Month Five, Tom will visit his customers and attempt to strengthen the bonds of their business relationship. During the first four months, he used his customer account cards (Chapter Ten) to note areas of common interest. In Month Five, he will reinforce these common interests. By doing so, he will separate himself from those cold and timid souls who are only interested in making the sale. Tom will also use these visits to remind his customers what makes XYZ so special. Remember, people like to do business with people who are like themselves. This month, Tom's goal is to demonstrate that he is "one of the gang."

Tom initially planned to use Month Five to launch a direct mail and telemarketing program providing his prospects with another special offer. Since he has hired Tina, however, he has decided to introduce her to his customers and potential customers. He will send out a mailer introducing Tina to his target audience. He will use the fact that she had been hired to project the image of a successful product and a prosperous business. Tom's implied message will be: "Because the demand for XYZ's self-calibrating widget has been so strong, I have had to add another person to the office. If we are this successful, then perhaps you should be using our product."

Figure Nine illustrates this mailer.

FIGURE NINE

Front of the XYZ Mailer

XYZ COMPANY
3224 Maple Lane
Boise, Idaho 30232

John Q. Public
3155 Main. Street
Boise, Idaho 30232

Back of the XYZ Mailer

XYZ COMPANY
PROUDLY ANNOUNCES
THAT TINA TAYLOR HAS JOINED US
AS A CUSTOMER SERVICE REPRESENTATIVE

TINA LOOKS FORWARD TO WORKING WITH YOU
BECAUSE CUSTOMER SATISFACTION IS HER JOB
AND OUR GOAL

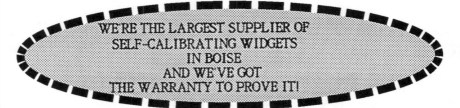

WE'RE THE LARGEST SUPPLIER OF
SELF-CALIBRATING WIDGETS
IN BOISE
AND WE'VE GOT
THE WARRANTY TO PROVE IT!

CALL TINA OR TOM AT **XXX-XXXX** FOR AND LET US DEMONSTRATE WHY OUR
BUSINESS MAKE SENSE FOR YOUR BUSINESS

Tom also plans to have Tina introduce herself to the target audience. He and Tina have agreed on the following telemarketing script:

"Hello. May I speak with_____. Hello. My
name is Tina Taylor and I wanted to introduce myself to you. I
was recently hired by Tom Tuttle and XYZ. As you probably
know, we are currently offering the longest widget warranty
of any supplier in Boise. My job will be to make certain that
our growing family of customers is a happy family of customers.
If I can answer any of your questions or be of any assistance,
please do not hesitate to call me. Thank-you for your time and
have a wonderful day."

A common sense sales campaign should possess the flexibility to take advantage of any opportunities which occur. Tom is using Tina's hiring to send a message that his business is growing. He is also letting his customers know how important customer service is to his company. It is so important, XYZ has decided to hire a full-time employee to handle it.

Month Six: Another Special Offer.

Month Six represents the midpoint of Year One. At the end of this month, Tom will review the success of his common sense sales program (Chapter Nine). He will do this to determine which techniques have been effective and what changes need to be made. I recommend that you reassess your battleplan at the end of Month Sixth. You need to know what you are doing right and what you are doing wrong. Remember, each market is different. One sales strategy may be highly successful while another might be a complete disaster. Discover what works in your marketplace so that you can maximize your success.

This month, Tom plans to unveil another special offer. His monthly mailer will offer customers and potential customers the opportunity to "Buy Ten Widgets And Get One Free." He will point out that an order of one thousand widgets would result in an additional one hundred free widgets. At the current price of $15.00 per widget, this represents a savings of $1,500.00. This offer will have a fixed expiration date. [As an exercise, I challenge you to place yourself in the role of Tom Tuttle. Attempt to sketch out what this mailer would look like if you were preparing it.]

Tom also plans to have Tina contact people two weeks after this offer has been sent to verify that they received it and to remind them that it is good until x/x/90. The real purpose of this reminder, however, is to increase the response rate of the special offer. Tom has decided to combine all future direct mail offers with a telemarketing follow-up. His goal is to increase the number of people who will use each of his special offers. And, while Tina is reminding people of the special offer, she will also remind them of what it is that makes XYZ so special (i.e., the USP).

WHERE DO I GO FROM HERE?

We focused on Tom Tuttle's common sense sales campaign during Months One through Six to examine how he applied the techniques and strategies covered in the previous chapters. The goal of Chapter Eight has been to provide you with an example of how these techniques and strategies can be utilized as part of a comprehensive common sense sales campaign. Remember, each individual and each market are different. Tom's program was designed to take advantage of his particular strengths and respond to the needs of his particular marketplace.

When you design your program, it should conform to your strengths and fit the needs of your marketplace. It should also conform to what you learn about your business environment (i.e., what will appeal to your heavy users and what you can offer them that your competition cannot). The litmus test is to ask yourself two very important questions. First, does this sales approach make sense for me? Second, does it feel comfortable? The essence of common sense selling is selling which is sensible and comfortable. It is the application of strategies and techniques which enable you to maximize your personal strengths while selling your product or service to others.

I have decided to leave Tom Tuttle and his fledgling operation at the end of six months because it is time for Tom to review what he did right and what he did wrong. Unless he has drastically underperformed his objectives, he should continue using the same theme and advertising the same USP during Months Seven through Twelve. What Tom may decide to alter, however, is his method of transmitting this USP.

Tom's direct sales, direct mail and telemarketing programs represent the means of transmitting his message and creating a "selling opportunity." These three tools are part of a larger common sense sales arsenal. This arsenal could include radio, television, outdoor advertising, sponsoring a special event, etc.

We did not explore these other tools because of the expense involved in their use. I assumed that your financial resources are limited and therefore selected three tools which, based on my experience, are cost effective. Nonetheless, at the end of six months, your assumptions and subsequently the tools you use to achieve your desired objectives may change in response to changes in your marketplace.

Let's assume that Tom's approach has been highly successful. His gains in Boise therefore would represent someone else's losses. The competition might decide it was time to offer a standard one-year warranty. Or, they might decide to raise the stakes by offering a standard two-year warranty. The point is: <u>you cannot formulate your common sense sales program in a vacuum.</u> At the end of six months, you need to evaluate the success of your program. You also need to reexamine your competition to determine what adjustments they have made to you and how you can respond to these changes. Like a chess player, each move on the board must be met by a countermove. Like a chess player, your goal is to capture your opponents players (or, in our case his customers). To accomplish this, you must periodically review your strategy and determine how it has altered the competitive environment within your marketplace.

Month Six is an excellent time to reevaluate your strategy. The more successful you have been, the greater the likelihood that your success has produced changes in your business environment. The question to be posed at the end of Month Six is: Where do I go from here? To answer this question, you need to examine where you have been and what you have accomplished. You also need to reexamine your business environment. I shall now present a plan for analyzing the success of your sales program.

# How to analyze the success of your sales program.

The process of analyzing the success of your sales program has two fundamental components. The first component is **goal-setting**. Prior to launching your common sense sales campaign, you need to develop objectives. These objectives can be expressed in terms of how many customers you capture, how many dollars you earn, how many units you sell, etc. My personal recommendation is that you use objectives which are measurable and understandable.

If you are an owner or a manager who is responsible for the profitability of a business or a department, you may also need to establish profit objectives. Establishing sales and profit objectives requires you to examine the big picture. You must determine the impact of both revenues and expenditures on your operation. In addition to *Common Sense Selling*, I encourage you to research other topics such as managing expenses, analyzing productivity, and improving performance. These factors will also determine your ultimate success or failure and you need to understand how they affect your business.

The second component is **performance monitoring**. This refers to your ability to monitor whether your common sense sales program is doing what you intend it to do. More specifically, performance monitoring means examining which elements of your sales program are working and which are not.

In this chapter, I will review each of these characteristics. Goal-setting and performance monitoring are two tools you can use to analyze the success of your sales program. My goal in this chapter is to focus on how you determine whether or not have a problem. And, if you do have a problem, what to do about it.

THE IMPORTANCE OF GOAL SETTING

Before I started my business, I developed a business plan. The purpose of this plan was to develop measurable and understandable objectives. My success or failure would be based on my ability to achieve these objectives. This process of goal-setting, however, did not begin when I purchased a business. Like most people, I have been setting goals all my life. In college, my goal was to acquire the skills and knowledge I would need to be successful in later life. And, I measured my success based on the grades that I received.

When I was hired by a large corporation to serve in their sales division, my success was based on my ability to achieve quantifiable objectives. Each year, I was given a performance evaluation which rated my ability to achieve goals in such areas as sales, market share, retail representation, etc.

The important point is: no matter what you do or how you do it, setting goals and comparing your actual performance to those goals is how you determine if you are doing it right. In the case of Tom Tuttle and XYZ, their goal was to achieve their sales and market share objectives in Boise. Let's examine how they did this.

Tom Tuttle's responsibility was to penetrate his market. He and his superiors decided that the best method for determining whether or not he was succeeding would be to develop a three year sales forecast. This forecast would project overall widget sales in Boise, Idaho. Based on these industry projections, XYZ would establish its market share requirements. Since product development and manufacturing responsibilities would be based at the home office, Tom's objectives would focus on his attainment of his sales and market share objectives. [Please Note-In this type of an operation, it would not be unusual for the home office to assign Boise a share of the variable costs of production based on their sales output. It would also not be unusual for Tom's costs to include any overhead or fixed costs incurred by his office. We will not, however, address this issue of assigning costs and determining profitability based on these costs because it is beyond the scope of our analysis.]

The question becomes: How does XYZ develop its forecast? One method is to examine what the market has done over the past several years and, based on economic assumptions regarding industry growth, project what the market will do over the next several years. Each industry publishes statistics on its sales. The U.S. Department of Commerce uses these figures to develop its own projections on industrial growth and productivity. You can obtain sales data on your particular industry by contacting the Department of Commerce and requesting one of their published reports. Or, you can examine your industry's trade publications. A local library or chamber of commerce may provide you with this information.

Before opening their office in Boise, Tom Tuttle and his superiors examined sales data on widgets. [For purposes of simplicity, let's assume that the self-calibrating widget is the only type of widget currently on the market.] They focused on widget sales in the Boise market. XYZ then examined what it considered to be reliable growth estimates of national widget sales and widget sales in Boise over the course of the next three years. Based on this data, XYZ developed its own forecast for widget sales in Boise during this period. Since the company's three year nationwide objective was to achieve a fifteen percent share of the industry, Tom was given the objective of achieving a fifteen percent share as well.

Tom was not, however, expected to achieve fifteen percent of his market overnight. His company, based on its experience in other markets, decided it would be realistic for Tom to capture a fifteen percent share of the Boise market by the end of his third year of operation. His company established a "stair-step" program in which he was assigned one, two and three year sales and market share goals. His goal was to achieve a seven percent share of his market by the end of Year One, eleven percent by the end of Year Two, and fifteen percent by the end of Year Three.

Figure Ten represents XYZ's forecast for the Boise market and Tom's sales objectives for Year One. These are measurable and understandable goals which Tom will use to evaluate his success in Boise. You may, however, be asking yourself the following question: If Tom's goals are based strictly on sales and share of market, then won't he risk jeopardizing XYZ's profitability in order to achieve his objectives? An excellent question. The answer is no. XYZ must approve any promotion or special offer before Tom is authorized to make it. In other words, the home office controls pricing and promotion decisions and is therefore able to ensure that its profitability goals are met. In your case, you must ensure that your profitability goals are met. Contrary to popular belief, you cannot lower your price below cost and make it up on the volume.

As indicated, Figure Ten represents Tom's market share and sales goals. We have included his actual sales data for the first six months of operation. He will use this data to analyze his sales performance. Chart One compares projected performance with actual performance. This chart is a graphic depiction of where Tom is versus where he ought to be. We can see in Figure Ten and Chart One that the Boise Office has underperformed its sales and market share objectives during the first five months of Year One. In Month Six, however, its sales experienced a significant increase and Tom succeeded in achieving an estimated 4.6% of his market versus an objective of 4%. This translates into an additional 1,800 units sold in Month Six.

What happened? One explanation is that the actual industry sales during Months One through Five were lower than XYZ projected. In this case, the lag between actual sales and projected sales could imply that Tom's market share performance will be revised upward. In other words, his actual performance could be better than the preliminary data suggests. It is also possible that his actual performance is worse than the preliminary data suggests. This will require further study.

A second possibility is that Tom's common sense sales campaign is taking a longer period of time to achieve the desired results than had been originally anticipated. In Month Six, however, the Boise Office outperformed its sales objectives. This could indicate that Tom is on the right track, but still needs to make some adjustments to his program. Six months of sales data is, by no means, conclusive. Nonetheless, when examined in conjunction with our second tool—performance monitoring—it can provide us with an indication of what, if any changes, need to be made in the program.

FIGURE TEN

XYZ COMPANY
FORECAST OF WIDGET SALES IN BOISE, IDAHO
YEAR ONE

	MONTH ONE	MONTH TWO	MONTH THREE	MONTH FOUR	MONTH FIVE	MONTH SIX	MONTH SEVEN
IND. SALES ESTIMATE	200,000	250,000	250,000	265,000	275,000	280,000	275,000
XYZ's % OF TOTAL MKT.	2%	3%	3%	4%	4%	4%	5%
# OF UNITS TO ACHIEVE MKT. SHARE REQUIREMENT	4,000	7,500	7,500	10,600	11,000	11,200	13,750
# OF UNITS ACTUALLY SOLD	2,000	4,000	6,500	9,000	10,000	13,000	
ACTUAL SHARE OF MKT.	1%	1.6%	2.6%	3.4%	3.6%	4.6%	

	MONTH EIGHT	MONTH NINE	MONTH TEN	MONTH ELEVEN	MONTH TWELVE	TOTAL-YEAR ONE
IND. SALES ESTIMATE	225,000	250,000	275,000	280,000	300,000	
XYZ's % OF TOTAL MKT.	5%	5%	6%	6%	7%	
# OF UNITS TO ACHIEVE MKT. SHARE REQUIREMENT	11,250	12,500	16,500	16,800	21,000	
# OF UNITS ACTUALLY SOLD						
ACTUAL SHARE OF MKT.						

Chart1

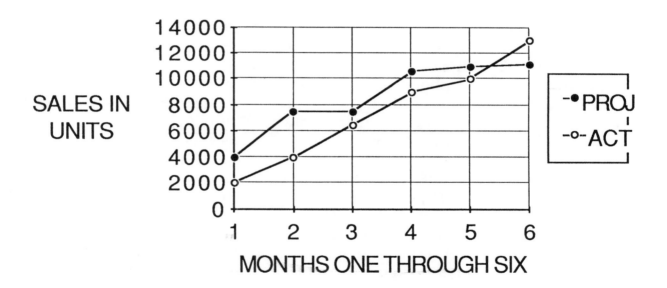

GRAPH ONE : XYZ BOISE OFFICE
PROJECTED VERSUS ACTUAL SALES

THE IMPORTANCE OF PERFORMANCE MONITORING

The process of setting measurable and understandable goals enables us to determine whether we are achieving these goals. If we are achieving or exceeding them, then we are on the right track. If not, then we have a problem. Goal-setting serves as an indicator which lets us know if, indeed, we do have a problem.

If we are failing to achieve the goals which we established, we can use performance monitoring to determine what is working and what isn't. Performance monitoring is a method of tracking the performance of our various selling mediums to determine what is effective.

In the case of Tom Tuttle, he has tracked his performance. On the invoice he uses to record each order, there is a place to indicate how the sale was made. Did Tom sell Ralph Torgensen of HIJ Company because of a face-to-face encounter, a telephone call, a mailer or a special offer. Each sale Tom made was made for a specific reason. On his invoice, Tom recorded what that reason was. Then, at the end of each month, he recorded this information on his Common Sense Selling Program Evaluation Form. This form is illustrated by Figure Eleven.

The aforementioned form is part of the paperwork process of your sales campaign. The reason I recommend you use this form or one like it is because common sense selling dictates that you know the dollar and unit value generated by each of the elements of your overall sales program. If, for example, Tom does a special offer or a telephone follow-up, he needs to know what the result of this offer or follow-up is in terms of widgets sold and revenues produced. By recording this information on his program evaluation form (Figure Eleven), he can review the results and make any necessary adjustments to his overall campaign.

Suppose that Tom discovers telemarketing appears to yield the highest results. It may be that it is easier to persuade decisionmakers in his marketplace over the telephone than in person. By increasing the number of telephone contacts and decreasing the number of person-to-person contacts, Tom should increase his sales. But, in order to do this, he needs to know how many widgets are being sold as a result of telemarketing and how many are being sold as a result of direct sales.

The process of performance monitoring through the use of program evaluation techniques is comparable to a baseball scout recording the box score of each player. By knowing who is hot and who is not, the scout is able to tell his manager who belongs in the lineup and who belongs on the bench. Like the baseball scout, if you set reasonable objectives and determine whether you are achieving those objectives, you will know if your team is winning or losing. If your team is losing, then you need to make changes in your lineup. A system of program evaluation enables you to make changes in your lineup which are not merely the result of guesswork.

The combination of goal-setting and performance monitoring will enable

FIGURE ELEVEN
COMMON SENSE SELLING PROGRAM EVALUATION FORM

DATE	BUSINESS NAME/ CUSTOMER NAME	TELEPHONE #	TYPE OF OFFER OR CONTACT	DOLLAR & UNIT VALUE

you to analyze the success of your sales program. You need to periodically revise your goals to respond to changes in your business environment. You also need to continually monitor performance because what works one month may not work the next. Like our baseball manager, you need to make regular changes in your lineup in order to build a winning team.

10 How to build a customer account system.

In Chapter Three, I reviewed the "rules of the game" of common sense selling. One of those rules was: Know Thy Prospect. This rule needs to be expanded to Know Thy Prospect and Know Thy Customer because your goal is to transform your prospect into a customer. To do this, you need to understand his business concerns and demonstrate how your product can address those concerns.

A problem often arises as your business grows. I encountered this problem as my business grew. My dilemma was that I began to lose touch with my old customers as I continued to pursue new ones. I asked myself the question, "How can I stay in touch with my customers while doing everything else that needed to be done?"

My answer was to develop a customer account system. This system enabled me to know whatever I needed to know about each of my customers. Instead of attempting to memorize a tremendous amount of information, I simply recorded important facts and reviewed this information prior to each contact. I developed a special customer account card which enabled me to record all of the relevant information about each of my customers and prospective customers. And, most importantly, this system proved to be a time-saving device because it permitted me to do everything else I needed to do.

My objective was not only to know the pertinent professional and personal facts about each account. I also needed to gauge each account's, or prospective account's, level of interest. After a contact, I would assess an individual's level of interest and record it on my customer account card. By doing so, I could evaluate whether a prospect had a low, moderate or high level of interest.

If an individual's level of interest was low, then I would periodically remind him that I was ready to serve his needs should his current supplier fail him. A periodic reminder might include a monthly mailer plus a telephone reminder once every three months. If his level of interest was moderate, then I would attempt to increase his level of interest by demonstrating that my product met his needs and that I cared about his business. This might involve a monthly mailer and a monthly phone call or visit. If his level of interest was high, then I asked for the order. I would request a meeting with the decisionmaker to discuss a long-term business relationship.

The role of each customer account card was twofold. First, it would provide me with the information I would need to know in order to build a relationship based on trust and likability. I would refamiliarize myself with the prospect prior to the contact to demonstrate that I knew who he was and that we had certain common areas of interest.

Second, I was able to review the level of interest. Prior to a contact, I would review the customer account card to determine the last time I spoke with my prospect and how interested he or she was at that time. By knowing the person's prior level of interest, I knew where to begin with each subsequent contact. For example, if the card indicated that the individual had expressed a low level of interest during the most recent contact then I would not begin by asking for the order. My system for tracking each individual, based on his level of interest, allowed me to adapt my approach to fit his current mood. When he was ready to buy, I was ready to sell. Consequently, this system reduced the likelihood of missed opportunities.

Figure Twelve is an example of the type of customer account card I developed. In the upper left hand corner, I would fill in the name, address, and telephone number of the business or organization. I also recorded the name of the decisionmaker (i.e., the man or woman who decided whether or not the organization did business with me) and the type of industry. I recommend classifying each prospect by business name and industry type. I also recommend filing out two cards for each prospective account. One card should be filed alphabetically by business name. The other alphabetically by industry type. This dual filing system provides you with the flexibility to focus your sales efforts on all heavy users or target specific users. You may discover a product feature or selling benefit which appeals to a specific type of business. By classifying businesses based on industry-type, it is therefore easier for you to develop industry-specific promotions.

In the upper right hand corner, I classified each prospect based on his level of interest. I suggest that you use a different colored dot for each category. Let's assume my prospect's level of interest is low. I would use a blue dot to signify this fact. When I glanced at his card, I would see the blue dot and instantly recognize that this prospect had a low level of interest. [Please Note-You may wish to distinguish between people already doing business with you and others whose business you are pursuing. I found it easier to simply classify a current account as someone who had a high level of interest and was therefore either doing business with me or was ready to do business with me.]

The advantage of using colored dots that can be adhered to each card is that it is easy to change these dots each time an individual's level of interest changes. In other words, you can continually adjust an account's level of interest to match your most recent contact.

It is also important to record people who have requested that you sever all communications with their business. Do not remove them from your file system, simply note their preference. Remember, even these people may change or be replaced with the passage of time. Some of my best accounts were businesses which initially indicated they wished to have no further communications with me. I advise you to recontact these accounts once every six months by mail or telephone

FIGURE TWELVE
FRONT OF THE CUSTOMER ACCOUNT CARD

Business Name_____

Type of Industry_____

Address_____

_____

Telephone Number_____

Decisionmaker_____

LEVEL OF INTEREST

○ HIGH
○ MODERATE
○ LOW
○ CUSTOMER
○ DEACTIVATE

DESCRIPTION OF KEY BUSINESS NEEDS

COMMON AREAS OF INTEREST WITH DECISIONMAKER

TYPE OF CONTACT/OFFER	DATE

FIGURE TWELVE
BACK OF THE CUSTOMER ACOUNT CARD

TYPE OF PURCHASE	VOLUME	DOLLAR AMOUNT

or both.

In Figure Twelve, below the name of the decisionmaker there is a box entitled "description of key business needs." The purpose of this box is to record your impressions of each prospect's "hot button." I define a person's "hot button" as the issue or issues of greatest concern. You need to know what appeals most to each account if you are to understand how to build a bridge between what you have to offer and what this decisionmaker needs to have. By recording this information on your card, each time you speak with this account, you are able to relate your product to his most immediate needs (e.g., quality, reliability, price). By doing so, you establish credibility because you become someone who appears to understand the needs of his customers.

The other advantage to knowing what is of greatest concern to your customers and prospective customers is that it gives you greater insight into their business. This is important because you may occasionally discover a new use for one of your products. This not only enhances your credibility, it increases your sales volume as well.

Below the "level of interest" there is a place to record any common areas of interest which you might have with someone. Remembering that people like to do business with people who are like themselves, this is good method for demonstrating that you are like them. I used this technique most effectively by making a casual reference to something I knew that I and the decisionmaker had in common. I then let him decide whether he wanted to pursue this topic of discussion. Whether he did or not, however, he was usually favorably impressed that I would take such a personal interest in him.

The lower third of the customer account card is to be used for recording each contact or offer that is made and the date when you made it. This information presents a concise history of your marketing relationship with each business. You can use it to pinpoint exactly when you last spoke with someone and whether or not they were receptive to a given offer. This information will also help you to determine how to establish the right type of business relationship with each of your accounts.

On the back side of the card is a history of the type, quantity and dollar volume of each purchase made by each customer. This information is important for a number of reasons. First, when you speak with a customer, you know this individual's purchasing history. Therefore, you are able to suggest a purchasing program that will serve both his needs and yours. You may discover you are able to offer your customer a high volume discount which will increase his savings and your revenues. Second, within each heavy user group there is usually a subgroup which represents your largest accounts. You need to know who these folks are and make certain you devote extra time to their needs. Third, the information on the purchasing history of an account can serve as an early warning system. If you notice that someone, who consistently does a high volume of business with you, has not placed an order with you in three months then you may have discovered a problem. Perhaps this individual was displeased by something. By detecting this, you may be able to stop him from taking his business elsewhere. But, do not be afraid to pick up a telephone and find out what is wrong. Your customers may not always tell you if they are unhappy about something. Nonetheless, if you take the time to find out and are willing to correct the problem, then you may avoid losing their business.

A customer account system should provide you with important information on the people who you want to do business with. It should be information which is useful and concise. It should also provide you with a brief history of your relationship with each decisionmaker. You will need to know: 1) Who is the decisionmaker, 2) What are his major concerns, 3) How interested is he in you and your product, 4) What do the two of you have in common, 5) What has been his purchasing history with you and 6) How you can do to continue to be his supplier. I believe that the customer account system outlined in this chapter will help you to answer these important questions.

How to manage customer satisfaction.

Let's assume that you have created a selling opportunity and applied the "rules of the game" of common sense selling to build a bridge between what you have to offer and what your prospect needs to have. You have made the sale and your prospect has become your customer. Now comes the hard part.

What distinguishes you from your competition may create an interested prospect. What you know about your prospect, your product and yourself may result in a sale. How you manage your customer—once he has become your customer—will, in all likelihood, determine your ultimate success. Your ability to maintain satisfied customers is the ultimate test of whether common sense selling will work for you. Without a program for managing customer satisfaction, everything else that you do will prove to be a waste of time.

Managing customer satisfaction implies demonstrating to your customers that you care about their business. In Chapter Nine, I emphasized the importance of analyzing success by setting goals and monitoring performance. In this chapter, I want to stress the importance of listening to your customers. In their book, *In Search of Excellence*, Peters and Waterman concluded that America's best run companies are successful because they listen to their customers. If you are to be successful, then you must listen to your customers.

The essence of an effective customer satisfaction program is one which enables you to listen and respond to whatever your customers are telling you. My advice is to implement a Customer Satisfaction Follow-Up Program. The objective of this program is to contact each customer to make certain that he or she is satisfied.

Each Friday, I suggest that you make a list of all of the people who did business with you during the previous week. You should record the following information: 1) the name of the customer, 2) the name of the business, 3) the telephone number of the business, and 4) the invoice or work order number. On the following Monday, you should call each of the people on this list. I suggest the following approach:

"Hello. May I speak with_____.
Hello. This is _____with_____
_____. I hope you had a pleasant weekend. The
reason I am calling you this morning is to thank you for doing
business with us. I realize that you had a choice and I am
grateful that you choose us. I also wanted to make certain that

you are completely satisfied."

You should contact every customer. Thank each one for the opportunity to serve his needs and make certain he is satisfied with the job you did for him. If you decide to try one idea I have presented in this book then this is the one. A program which lets your customers know you care is a program that will provide you with the foundation for repeat business.

If you are tempted to dismiss this idea as silly or irrelevant, then I challenge you to take a moment to list all of the people you have done business with over the past five years who have taken the time follow-up their work with a telephone call. Most people forfeit this golden opportunity to let their customers know they really care. If you seize this opportunity, then you will demonstrate to all who do business with you that you are someone who is worth doing business with.

Your customer satisfaction program also lets you know if you are doing a good job. It is the most effective method I know for avoiding serious problems and guaranteeing satisfied customers. Remember, common sense selling dictates that happy customers will come back again and again and again.

Figure Thirteen is an example of a Customer Satisfaction Log Sheet. I used this type of a log for my business. Each Friday I, or my Customer Service Manager, recorded the names, telephone numbers and invoice numbers of people we had done business with the previous week. On Monday morning, each of these people were contacted. When asked if they were satisfied with the work we had done, their comments were recorded on the log sheet. If there was a problem, it was noted. I reviewed this log each week and contacted any customers who had reported problems. Usually, I was successful in resolving these problems. Often, they were simply misunderstandings that resulted from a breakdown in communication. Whatever the reason, I had the opportunity to demonstrate to my customers that I cared. And this program enabled me to minimize potential customer losses.

I cannot overemphasize the importance of a program for managing customer satisfaction. All your efforts and energies in capturing customers can be undone if your are unable to retain these customers. I believe this program, if properly implemented, will enable you to keep your customers happy.

CUSTOMER FOLLOW-UP LOG SHEET

DATE_____

REPRESENTATIVE_____

BUSINESS/ DECISIONMAKER	SPOKE WITH	TEL #	INVOICE #	CUSTOMER COMMENTS	FURTHER ACTION REQUIRED

No one said it would be easy.

In Chapter One, I stated that I had not uncovered some secret formula or hidden concept enabling you to become wealthy beyond your wildest dreams. In all fairness, I should not conclude *Common Sense Selling* without introducing at least one idea which may change your life. In my travels, I have uncovered one concept that has consistently made a difference. This idea has provided me with a comfortable living throughout most of my adult life. I have tried to think of a way to express this powerful concept as an elaborate theory or impressive doctrine. Unfortunately, I have found this to be an impossible task. Therefore, I will describe my not-so-secret idea in simplest terms:

That's right. No one said it would be easy. So, allow me to be the first one to tell you that it's not easy. It's hard work!

The successful application of your common sense sales program will require you to work long and hard to achieve your desired objectives. This book offers no short-cuts. If you are looking for a short-cut to wealth, then try the lottery. To succeed with this program, you must be willing to do what it takes to be successful. This means you must be willing to invest your time, energy and effort in whatever program you devise.

If anyone tells you he has uncovered a program which will enable you to achieve great success with minimal effort, don't you believe it! Your odds of achieving one hundred percent success with zero percent effort are about as good as your odds of winning the ten million dollar lottery. Nothing in life that is truly worth having comes without some effort. No pain, no gain.

If you are willing to make the effort, then I believe *Common Sense Selling* will work for you. You must, however, invest the time and energy necessary to create your opportunity, sell your product and satisfy your customer. Remember, there are no short-cuts or free rides. This book can change your life only if you believe it can change your life. I offer the tools. You must do the job.

I began by telling you that *Common Sense Selling* was not intended to change your life. I shall conclude by telling you that this book can change your life. But only if you possess the desire and determination to make it happen.

I offer the tools. You must do the job.

Go for it!

THE END